A 'Be Abuse Aware'
"coercive and controlling behavic

http://www.beabuseaware.co.uk

"You are not obliged to accept abuse from anyone; whether they are your family, friend, or partner".

Written, published and book design by Stephen Cooke
The contents of this booklet will be continuously updated

Be Abuse Aware - Abuse
Version 1.7

First Published;
Paperback - May 2021, Hardcover - Dec 2021

ISBN: 9798508400118

With special thanks to the contributors, and artists at www.pixabay.com for the royalty-free images used.

This book is used in conjunction with volunteers within Domestic Abuse Charities as part of their work to help individuals, professionals, and families understand what abuse is and how it is maintained. This book can also be used as a self-help study guide aimed at identifying abuse. It is not a replacement for accredited training or support from professionals and studying this with a trusted friend is recommended.

- An isolated incident does not indicate abuse.

Please consider making a donation. The more awareness we spread, the safer the world is for everyone.

There are numerous charities and organizations that help with domestic abuse, these are listed later in this book. Be Abuse Aware is an information service only. We supply awareness books and help individuals and families access and engage in the required support and legal systems that are available within the UK. This book is part of a series of books aimed at awareness and recovery. If you're using this book independently, please try to use it as part of a group or with another person to gain the full benefits. Victims need to have a sense of validation regarding their feelings. Knowing the ways perpetrators employ, can help to alleviate any confusion surrounding the behavior. We hope this will increase awareness and allow more professionals to recognize and safeguard vulnerable people.

Society's understanding of domestic abuse is still very limited. Many emotionally healthy people simply cannot understand why a victim would put up with such behavior and some struggle to comprehend abuse that isn't physical. In our own experience, professional services are often lacking in the very understanding needed to identify covert abuse.

Abuse is often such a vicious personal attack upon the victim, that they are left mentally broken. Abuse is a process. It often starts subtle and takes time for the perpetrator to wear someone down until they are isolated and dependent on their abuser. Victims are often unable to make sense of what has happened. Confused and often traumatized, they will suffer significant harm alongside angry outbursts and acts that are completely out of their character. The Domestic Abuse Bill, sections 76 & 77 now recognizes reactive abuse (more on this later)."

Identifying and validating the abuse is pivotal for allowing victims to start the process of moving on, as well as being fully aware of what is right and wrong for the future.

The purpose of this book is to allow both victims and professionals to understand Covert and Controlling behavior. This will also help to understand and identify the difference between the victim and the perpetrator of abuse.

Written by survivors, for survivors and professionals alike.

"Please help us to understand who is to blame!"

IMPORTANT NOTICE

The book is written in the worst-case scenario for each topic to better aid understanding.

Abuse and personality disorders are all perceived as a scale from good to bad. Some traits are considered healthy at one end, and abusive at the other. Always consult a professional in abuse and never deal with abusers one on one unless trained and accredited to do so. Many IDVA's or Domestic Abuse Support workers will be more than willing to help. Including your local council who have domestic abuse coordinators who can assist you.

Contents

What is **Abuse**?

Introduction

Coercive abuse makes life very confusing for victims. Please be under no delusion, victims will have endured profound anguish and trauma. Abuse can be physical, psychological, emotional, sexual, financial, or social abuse. In law, Domestic Abuse is defined as being in an intimate or family relationship.

This type of abusive behavior is often a means of gaining power and control over another person. By gradually wearing someone down and changing the boundaries, an abuser will mold their victim into conforming to their ideals. As a result, victims become a shadow of their former selves, unable to perform simple self-care routines for fear of being attacked verbally or physically. Coercion is making another party act in an involuntary manner – under duress – by the use of threats, lies, or force.

Statistics indicate that women make up 85% of the victims of domestic abuse (Kershaw et al 2008). Domestic abuse is generally seen as both a cause and consequence of gender inequalities in society. However, it is important to recognize that anyone can experience domestic abuse, regardless of their gender, age, race, ethnic or religious group, class, sexuality, disability, or lifestyle. The government's definition of domestic abuse has recently been extended to include anyone over the age of 16 within the Domestic Abuse bill 2021. In the past, it covered people aged 18+.

The wide range of tactics abusers employ are used to make the victim feel less than, to diminish their self worth and gain ultimate control over them. Although men are more commonly the abuser it can happen to anyone regardless of age, gender, or sexuality. Abusers may use intimidation, threats and often project their own wrongdoing onto others. When someone realizes they are a victim of domestic abuse, they will try to 'fix' things or apply boundaries in an attempt to stop or reduce the abuse. The abuser reacts to this. They may threaten to hurt you or those in your care in order to maintain their control. During this phase of enlightening, it is vitally important to have a support network in place. It is far more desirable to remove yourself or the victim from the abuser's control completely. This is nearly always the professionals preferred approach.

Domestic abuse is different for everyone and alongside the acts of violence that cause physical harm or injury, many victims will also experience verbal abuse, name-calling, habitual criticism, insults, yelling, and shaming. Abusers are also experts at the use of underhanded emotional manipulation tactics that the victim may not be aware of. This is the covert and intentional infliction of psychological harm. Abusing by proxy is when the perpetrator of abuse will gain the help of a mutual friend, family member, or simple manipulation of a third party, to help them abuse the victim by name-calling, controlling, or berating them. A newer term circulating on social media which is used to describe this type of harm is 'flying monkeys' however the two are slightly different with abuse by proxy being more harmful. This is normally done by telling them how 'bad' you are, and asking them to help the victim understand their bad behavior.

Many 'flying monkeys' believe the abuser and could also believe they are helping. But it can also be the case, that they are actually aware and either enjoying the 'drama' or are simply siding with them. This is often the case in families where the old saying blood is thicker than water comes into play. These types of families are especially dangerous as they will also encourage (either consciously or subconsciously) abusive behavior. Use this program to help you understand who is the abuser, and who is the victim. It is not always the case that both parties have some responsibility in arguments, "it takes two" can be misleading and actually cause more harm than good. In an abusive relationship, it is common for only the perpetrator to be at fault. Reactions to abuse, even extreme reactions are trauma responses and should be handled as such.

It's also very important to realize the difference between reactive abuse and perpetrators' abuse. Often there are reasons behind the abuse, such as childhood trauma, being drunk, or having a bad day. These causes cannot be used as an excuse for the perpetrator's behavior. Their behavior stems from a need to control and dominate their partners, you may even find yourself excusing abuse based on the past the perpetrators may have suffered. While these underlying causes can be examined to help understand the behavior, these reasons cannot be used to justify it. Abuse is rarely caused by a lack of self-control and often is a deliberate choice that is made. Remember their public face is a friendly and charming one, most of the time.

The abuse is most often manifested through underlying mental health issues such as a lack of self-worth, psychological issues, learned behavior, traditional ideas, and/or drinking and drugs.

TASK.

Discuss your own experiences of abuse with your volunteer or friend.

1. Are there any occasions that confuse you, and why?

2. How many types of abuse can you think of?

3. What is important for you to gain from this program?

4. Who in your opinion is most likely to be an abuser, and to whom?

Behaviours associated with potential abuse

Many of us show behaviours which could be identified as abusive, especially on off days. The following attributes are red flags but people who show them are not necessarily abusers. Frequently showing these behaviours however, or carrying them to the extreme should be viewed as potential abusive behaviour.

- Past Patterns of abuse
- Aggression during sex or playful use of force during sexuality
- Cruelty to animals and children
- Consistent blame
- hypersensitivity
- concern as control
- Jealousy
- moving to quickly

Physical Abuse.

Physical abuse can include many different types of assault. They may physically hit, punch, kick, spit or slap their victim. More serious assaults such as strangling and burning as well as physically restraining, pushing, pulling hair and/or using weapons can also be employed. In the Domestic Abuse bill 2021, it clearly states that violence or abuse against a partner for the sexual gratification of either party is not a defense when brought to court. These types of assaults do often increase in severity over time and the more the abuser is allowed to inflict his/her abuse, the more long term damage can be caused. Simply allowing the perpetrator to get away with bad behaviour, simply for ease or to 'not cause an argument' will have the effect over time of increasing their abusive behaviour in nearly all circumstances. Medical studies have also identified domestic abuse as a factor in serious brain injuries (Corrigan et al 2003) as well as physical injuries such as broken bones and bruising (Campbell 2002).

It is important to remember that it is not just the physical contact with the victim, perpetrators of abuse may also 'demonstrate' their physical dominance by punching walls and furniture or assaulting pets and other family members. Abusers often behave in a hostile, loud and "in your face", aggressive manner to intimate and force your compliance. Victims will often feel like any argument could be their last, normally arguments can be healthy and are a normal part of any relationship.

They are used to resolve issues, but abusers will make it very clear that negative conversations will not just jeopardize the relationship but may actually result in the victim being punished. Once the cause of the argument has been settled, it should not be kept up, and giving each other space and privacy is normal. From an early age, most of us are taught how to spot the signs of physical abuse such as broken bones or bruising enabling us to identify when we or our friends are being mistreated. But with covert abuse it's not obvious at all and if this is suspected, never disregard it. There are various signs of physical abuse, it's important to note here that in most cases, physical abuse is often done to parts of the body not visible to others.

Physical abuse includes;

Bruises (particularly if the individual can not be clear about how the bruising happened). The most obvious are on the face. Black eyes or bruised cheeks.

Broken bones. Survivors of physical abuse who experience broken bones may have a history of more than one broken bone. X-rays will likely show fractures or breaks in various stages of healing.

Burns. This is a common type of physical abuse. Cigarette burns, burns or blisters from scalding water or grease burns that cover a large area of the body, hand burns from hobs or naked flames.

Head injuries. A concussion is a common sign of physical abuse. Again being evasive about how the injury occurred could be a warning sign.

TASK.

1. What other signs of physical violence can you think of?

2. How could someone hide the signs of abuse?

3. What would raise your own suspicions that someone was not being truthful and hiding their injuries?

4. Who would you tell if you had concerns about abuse?

Rage and the Cycle of Abuse.

The rage of an abuser is often referred to as 'narcissistic rage' on social media. This rage is often directed at the victim, but is a projection of the abusers mood and confusion on the inside. The arguments of an abuser can last from hours to days before calming down. The Cycle of Abuse is a theory developed by Lenore Walker in her book, The battered Woman from 1979. This cycle is similar to the power and control wheel described later. This cycle is described as having four stages: Tension Building, Incident, Reconciliation and Calm. Each stage is defined by certain characteristics.

Tension-Building. This is the stage where the abuser is triggered and his/her tension builds. It could have nothing to do with the victim and include stresses of daily life, work, bills or conflict over ex partners or children. Again there are deeper concerns such as the risk factors in domestic abuse covered later.

Incident. This phase is where the incidents of explosive rage or violence, emotional, psychological or other forms of abuse erupt. The perpetrator will use any elements he can think of to control and dominate his victim. Often (but not all the while) using anger and/or violent outbursts and projecting anything they could do themselves onto the victim. Abusers will often blame the victim for wrongs they have thought about doing themselves.

Reconciliation. This is where the rage has calmed down and the abuser will start to make excuses and apologies, often called the 'honeymoon' period. Often showing remorse and begging for forgiveness they blame anyone and anything for their reactions. Promising this will never happen again, that they will seek help and even try to blame the victim for provoking their actions, diminishing and sweeping under the carpet everything that has happened during the incident or the extent of the harm that was caused. Gaslighting is often massively engaged at this point.

Calm. This is the time when things are relatively calm and peaceful. Love-bombing is used and the abuser may even carry out some of the promises to seek help or change. As time goes on the abuser however falls back into the cycle, showing less and less effort in their behavior and the demands and stresses of everyday life begin the tension-building phase again.

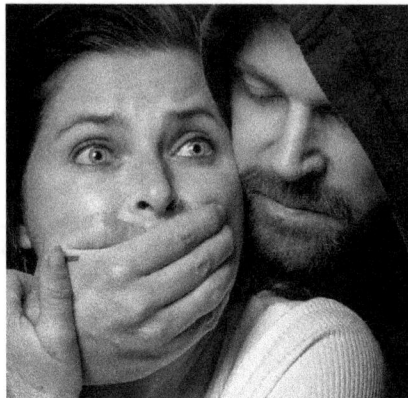

TASK.

Can you identify with any of these stages? Can you imagine how this would play out between an abuser and a victim. Using the graphic below or a separate sheet of paper, create a brief example of each stage.

Tension building, the incident, what happened and what was said during the reconciliation stage, and how it would feel during the calm stage. Do you think the victim's feelings during the calm stage would make you more agreeable to bad behavior?

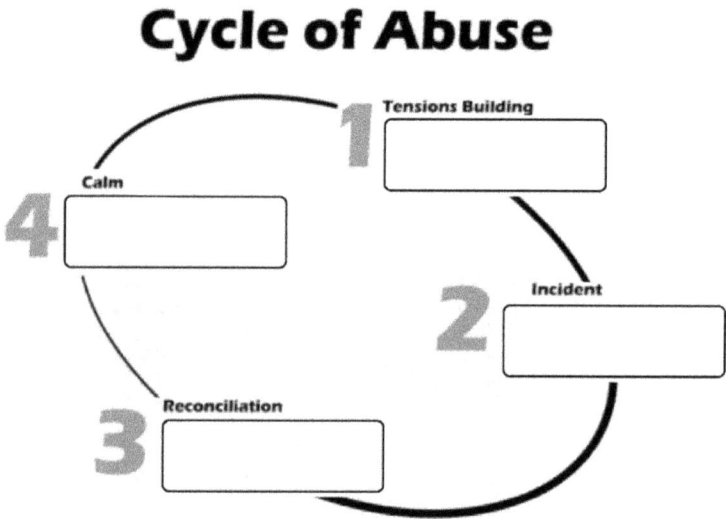

Cycle of Abuse

Tensions Building

Calm

4

1

Incident

2

Reconciliation

3

Do you know the difference between the cycle of cbuse, and the cycle of abusive relationships?

Emotional & Psychological Abuse.

Where physical abuse often leaves physical evidence, emotional abuse tends to be more hidden, subtle, and a far more sophisticated form of domestic abuse. This makes it far harder to recognize and take legal action against. Through personalized idealisation and subtle devaluation abusers can erode the identity of any victim. Often victims are highly intelligent. The intentions of the perpetrator are the same as other types of domestic abuse because they are seeking to control, degrade, humiliate and punish the victim. Emotional and physiological abuse can cause lasting trauma where the effects cannot be minimized affecting a person's everyday life to such an extent normal tasks can become impossible. Often memory lapses and confusion are signs of this trauma. The detailed effects of abuse are detailed in chapter 2 of this book.

Tactics of emotional abuse vary greatly and not all of them can be covered in detail. Discuss with your volunteer the types of emotional abuse you believe first starting you thinking something wasn't right, and keep notes if you need to. It is very common for emotional abuse to include the use of threats; for instance a perpetrator may threaten to take the children or report the victim to Social Services as an unfit parent, threaten to or actually harm a family member if the victim leaves or says that they will kill themselves if the relationship ends.

It is also extremely common for the perpetrators' control over their victims to continue well after any physical separation. It's important to understand that healing can only start when this influence is no longer present.

Read these examples;

- I will report you to the police,
- I will report you to Social Services,
- I will report you to the Benefits agency,
- I will tell 'someone' about how you're abusing me,
- 'someone' is going to beat you up or kill you,
- I will not let you have any money,
- I will tell others you're lying about 'something',
- I will make your kids hate you,
- I will take your kids away from you,
- I will tell everyone you hit me,
- I will tell everyone your crazy so no one will believe you,
- I will make you homeless,
- I will stop you from seeing your friends or family,
- I will destroy this family,
- I will have you committed (to a mental hospital),
- If you post anything on 'social media' I will make trouble or argue,
- I will embarrass you in public,
- Telling you to comply or there is 'no telling what I will do',
- I will hurt the children unless you do this,
- If you do that, then I will hurt the children.

can you think of three more?

1.
2.
3.

Have any of these been used against you personally? Talking about these with others can help the victim gain a sense of validation that their experience was real, something which is so often denied to them by the perpetrators.

Perpetrators will try to isolate the victim as a form of control. This will include friends and family by 'discouraging' them from going out or contacting family and friends. This is sometimes done by attacking the integrity and character of friends and family or arguing over the smallest of things to 'punish' you subconsciously for even daring to have your own life. Your hobbies or even work are very often discouraged and the sense of choice and control over your own life is undermined because you are often excluded from making important decisions. As we have already touched on how living with everyday threats of violence and emotional abuse has the most devastating effects on survivors. It can be argued that it's easier to live with emotional abuse than the physical abuse, as there are no outward signs. There are signs that a person has suffered emotional abuse.

Some of these are;

• The person feels afraid to speak their mind,
• They hate asking for help,
• They bury their emotions,
• They view their own needs as a burden,
• They need everything to be perfect,
• They feel ignored if they do speak up,
• They have a harsh inner critic,
• Any form of criticism is triggering and overwhelming.

TASK.

For each of the following, give 3 examples of how perpetrators would achieve their goal;

1. Isolation,
2. Making jokes that are actually insulting,
3. Catastrophism (Making a mountain out of a molehill!),
4. Guilt Tripping.

Love-Bombing & Flattery

When a relationship with an abuser starts, it's common for things to move extremely fast. Abusers can already have a lot of information about you from your social media or friends. For instance what you have in common, your likes, dislikes and where you like to go. This is how they pretend to be perfect for their victim. They will attempt to mirror the victims hopes, dreams and past hurt. Using their insecurities and loneliness to form an immediate bond of trust. They may be very overwhelming and initiate communication on every level, flooding your social media or texts with love, poems, songs, compliments, and inside jokes to put off penitential suitors. Abusers also have an endless list of pity plays and sob stories for them both to bond over. Often they don't know themselves what they actually want. They also make a point of telling you their good traits, not letting you spot them on your own.

They say drama is not their thing, but often there's more drama around them than anywhere else. This type of behavior is often used at the beginning of a relationship or when they feel they are losing control of the victim. As with most of the advice in this book, abuse is not a tick box exercise. Depending on the emotional intelligence of the abuser and their experiences, instead of love-bombing, they may try to force you into submission using threats or bad behavior. There are moments in this phase when they're cute and charming. This person who they fell in love with, often does not actually exist. This persona is easily replaced by something else entirely. The victim may even be scared by the emotional emptiness of the 'devil eyes', the cold manipulative, and inconsiderate thing that slips through. The victim will feel something isn't right but won't be able to put their finger on it until later.

TASK.

Do you think there are any tell-tale signs you could look out for during this stage in a new relationship? Read the following and see how many you can add. No one is perfect and having a few of these is normal but too many and it's a deal-breaker.

These can be difficult to spot if you are unaware.

1. They have cheated on a past partner,

2. They push your boundaries in 'innocent' ways,

3. They rush a new relationship far too quickly,

4. They try to isolate you from friends and family,

5. They hold you to double standards,

6. All their previous partners are 'crazy',

7. They call you names in arguments,

8. They make you feel confused or stupid,

9. They cannot stop saying just how perfect you are,

10. They refuse to work, without a reason,

11. They're cruel to their parents or strangers,

12. There secretive about things,

13. They demand to have your passwords and phone,

14. They guilt trip you every chance they get,

15. They make fun of you,

16. They 'roll' their eyes at you a lot,

17. They refuse to make your relationship public,

18. Their mood can change in an instant,

19. They're incapable of saying sorry.

Trauma Bonding & Name-Calling.

Trauma bonding is often associated with Stockholm syndrome. Although similarities exist between the two, especially in the context of developing an emotional bond with the victim, they are distinct from one another. The main difference is the directionality of the relationship. Stockholm syndrome is actually extremely rare. Trauma-bonding isn't. Stockholm syndrome can develop when victims of abuse believe their is a threat to there physical or psychological survival, and they also believe their abusers would carry out that threat.

"If Jane was trauma-bonded to John. Jane has an emotional bond and 'loves' John. John, however, just uses Jane for what he can get. In Stockholm syndrome, John would also have developed an emotional bond with Jane also."

Stockholm syndrome develops when people are placed in a situation where they feel intense fear of physical harm and believe all control is in the hands of their tormentor. The psychological response follows after a period of time and is a survival strategy for the victims. It includes sympathy and support for their captor's plight and may even manifest in negative feelings toward officers who are trying to help the victims. Situations in which the victims have displayed this kind of response have included hostage situations, long-term kidnappings, members of cults, prisoners of concentration camps, and more. With Stockholm syndrome, victims have been known to continue living a life of 'condition-ment' even after the relationship has ended.

Both trauma-bonding and Stockholm syndrome require specialist counseling.

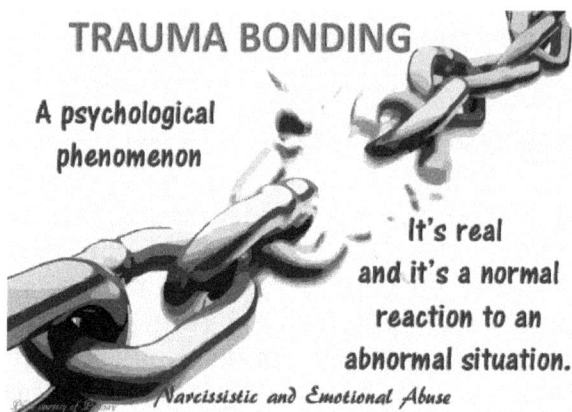

TRAUMA BONDING

A psychological phenomenon

It's real and it's a normal reaction to an abnormal situation.

Narcissistic and Emotional Abuse

Image Credit: http://narcissisticandemotionalabuse.co.uk/

Trauma bonding is complex and further research and professional counseling is recommended if you suspect this, often C-PTS is also an issue. The way that victims are treated can vary between relationships. These are some examples.

Everyday decisions such as where to live or how to decorate your home or the make of the car you drive are taken out of your hands. Often you are unaware of how this has happened and you agree to keep the peace. One emotional technique the perpetrator uses is being highly critical of the victim. They will blatantly call you names such as 'stupid', 'loser', 'lazy', or other words much too offensive to put into text. The perpetrator becomes not only the giver of the abuse but also able to take away the abuse or protect you from the abuse. They are able to prevent the threatened action if you do as you're told.

The passive/aggressive cycle used to achieve this trauma bond is easy to miss due to the confusion it creates. One minute they will shower you with attention, another they will ignore you or criticize you. Of course, the 'public' image is always maintained and they will treat you differently in public than behind closed doors.

Abusers will actively put in as little effort as possible and only engage more when you try to disengage. Spotting all these signs (red flags) early on will prevent the victim from falling into another abusive relationship out of the need to be accepted. Trauma bonding leaves a lasting impression almost like a drug dependency and unless treated as such, victims are doomed to repeat abusive relationships.

Abusive relationships are very often one-sided. The saying 'it takes two to tango', or 'you must have done something to deserve it' often does not apply and can not only be a form of abuse by proxy but invalidates the victim's experience causing lasting harm. The dominant traits of an abusive relationship are control and power. The perpetrator wants complete control over the victim. This normally happens slowly. It's important to remember that most relationships do not start off abusive and if you take the traits of a narcissist it is widely believed the 'mask' of Mr Nice guy will slip in around 6 months or less of contact. If the victim develops a bond as a coping mechanism (also remember most abusers are not 100% abusive, 100% of the time), they will often remember this 'loving' bond and start accepting the abuse because they want to get this loving and caring person back. It's important to understand that the most effective way abusive people control their partners is through this bond. Break the Silence has a separate module dedicated to this type of abuse.

The Power and Control Wheel was developed by the Domestic Violence Intervention programs in Minnesota, US, and is now widely used throughout the world in helping victims of domestic abuse to highlight the tactics used by abusers.

TASK

1. Describe the main difference between Trauma-bonding and Stockholm Syndrome.

2. Describe 3 situations that an abuser could use to create a trauma-bond?

3. Does a victim who is Trauma-bonded want help? Why?

The Power and Control Wheel

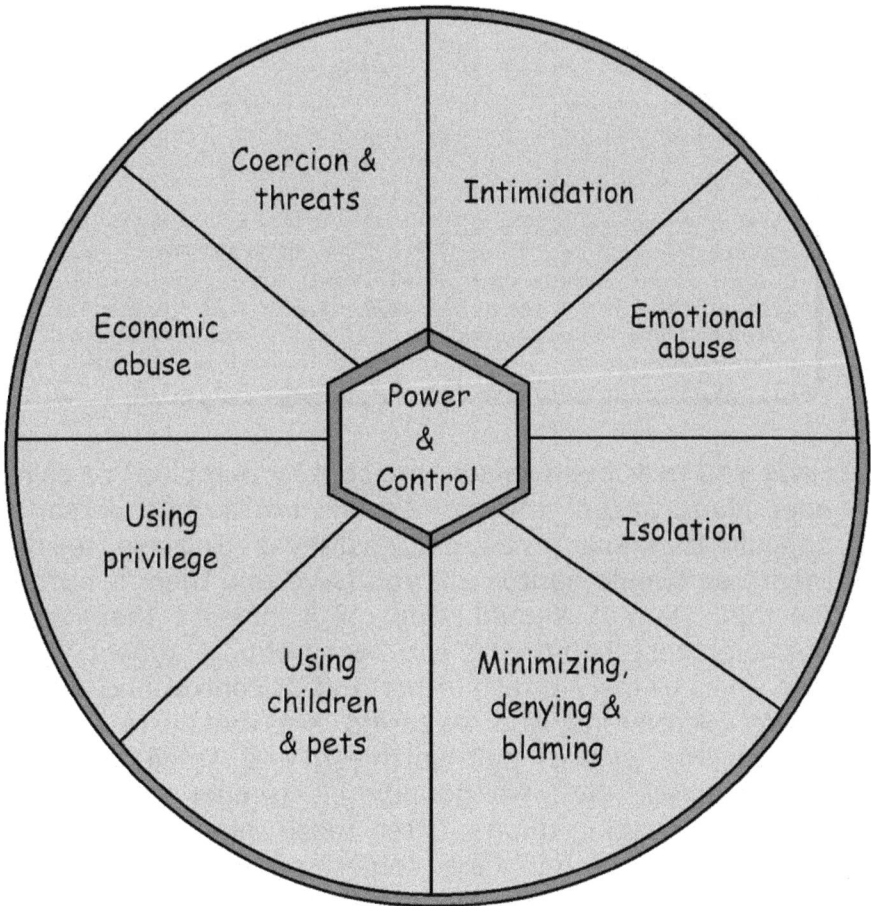

Character assassination, and Circular Conversations.

Bullying! Its extremely common for abusers to use derogatory names or 'character assassination' techniques.

Have you ever been called "my chubby pumpkin" or called an ape? Made to feel undermined and not a good person. It is difficult to know in all circumstances if these terms are meant as simple banter – if you have told them it hurts your feelings, then it should stop. If it doesn't then it's very possible these comments can be emotional abuse. Yelling is also an extremely effective method of control and emotional abuse. Screaming and swearing are meant to intimidate, making the victim feel worthless and small – it's often accompanied by fist-pounding, temper tantrums or throwing/breaking things. Often these rage's are in response to trying to communicate something, but your views are dismissed and you are made to feel it's not important. This can be done in a number of ways such as eye-rolling, smirking, head shaking or telling you that this 'subject' is just beyond your understanding.

A perpetrator will dismiss their actions as a 'joke' and attempt to make you look foolish for reacting. Often comparing the victim to others in their life such as ex-lovers, friends, or family. This is called devaluing and is used to make the victim feel jealous and inferior. Idealizing/love-bombing is the opposite and the victim is made to feel better than anyone else he/she knows. The very qualities the abuser once claimed they loved, have now become glaring faults and the victim will try and address these, spending more and more time trying to prove they are the very same person as the abuser once 'fell in love with. Always remember that an abuser's weapon of choice is word salad! Just when you think you have something worked out, you're forced to begin discussing it again in two minutes! Reciting everything that has already been said. The abuser uses the same garbage and random arguments and ignores any legitimate arguments or concerns you have. The resolution will be on their terms only, and if you have genuine worries such as why they're on the phone, why they're eager to get off the phone when you're there and you bring this up. It will be like you have never talked about it before. They will make you feel crazy or high maintenance and blame you, saying they're sick of arguing about this. It's basically a conversation from hell. They will throw one thing after another at you, not actually saying anything, but talking at you. These arguments will have your head spinning and can cause serious damage! Disengage as much as you can to prevent that mental harm! Arguments can be very hard to resolve due to the inability to get across anything they have done wrong. If you point out something they're doing, they'll start recounting the numerous unrelated things that you have done wrong in the past. Then using these to compare their actions to yours. "My cheating isn't as bad as what you did!", or "you can't complain about it because". It is very hard and time-consuming going through this type of situation, you could go hours or days replaying the argument, obsessing over it. You will feel drained and can be left with an actual headache!

This repeated behaviour slowly and steadily erodes away any boundaries you once had. Abusers groom you into accepting their bad behaviour as the 'norm'. Teasing becomes the primary mode of communication in the relationship. Belittling the victims intelligence and abilities, but if this is pointed out it's the victim who is the crazy one and they learn to push away these feelings to 'keep the peace', in essence becoming numb. The victim will constantly be on edge, or walking on eggshells around the abuser. This situation will keep the victim in a state of fight or flight, also known as hyper-arousal or an acute stress response. This state causes a hormonal cascade within the brain, especially norepinephrine and epinephrine. Being in this state for a prolonged period leads to long-term mental health problems. Depression, anxiety and PTSD among a few. Treatment for trauma is recommended. It's very common for the victim to try and come up with a diplomatic solution, where the blame is often split between the parties so you can both apologize. Victims of domestic abuse will often find they are the ones doing all the apologizing.

TASK

1. Assign yourself a role, abuser or victim. Then get someone else to take on the role of the other.
2. Its the 'abusers' turn to take out the trash but they have just been sitting down watching TV. The victim has asked them to take out the trash for the 3rd time and an argument starts.
3. Play out the conversation they have, but the abuser creates a circular conversation.
4. Try to include misdirection, blame, belittling and devaluing.

Accomplishments, interests and minimisation.

> ## Minimisation (psychology)
>
>
> From Wikipedia, the free encyclopedia
> (Redirected from Belittle)
>
> **Minimisation** or **minimization** is a type of deception[1] involving denial coupled with rationalisation/rationalization in situations where complete denial is implausible. It is the opposite of exaggeration. Minimisation, or downplaying the significance of an event or emotion, is a common strategy in dealing with feelings of guilt.[2] Words associated with minimisation include:

Always remember, you are important. No-one has the right to insult your appearance, say your hair is ugly or your outfit horrible! These types of insults are again aimed at undermining your self image, your choices and ultimately your control. Perpetrators will belittle your accomplishments and say your achievements mean nothing, often claiming responsibility for any success you have. "I made you, I can destroy you" is a quote often used. They will put down your interests saying they are worthless, stupid and a waste of time. They could say your out of your league, even telling you they are protecting you from looking stupid. Be fully aware, perpetrators will know what annoys you, and they will bring it up again and again any chance they get. They might try to embarrass you in public or in front of friends and will lecture you in front of others about all the things you do wrong or have outbursts in public. Never allow someone else to tell you how to feel, or who you are! Often an abuser will provoke jealousy or rivalries while maintaining their own innocence. After the love-bombing phase where they have been directing all their attention towards the victim, it can be very confusing when they withdraw and focus on someone else. After such a beautiful and emotionally focused start to the relationship these rivalries are encouraged because of the need for "supplying the drama" abusers crave.

TASK

Have you ever been so proud of something and another person has put you down, or "put you in your place"?

1. How did it make you feel?

2. Did it have to be said at all?

3. How did you respond?

Image: clipartsworld.com

Monitoring, Spying, and financial control.

It is often the case with abusive relationships which are 'toxic' that monitoring your whereabouts is a real issue. They will want to know where you are at all times. Insist that you respond to calls and texts immediately and might even show up where you're supposed to be. This is controlling behaviour, but also being aware of the other person's past can mitigate this behaviour. It may be they act like this for a reason other than being controlling or abusive, such as they have been abused themselves in the past, cheated on, abandoned or lost a loved one.

If their behaviour is causing you to be unhappy, scared or isolated then this is a problem that needs addressing. Often this monitoring will include digital means such as checking your internet history, emails or texts. Going as far as demanding your passwords and if you don't tell them accusing you of hiding something just so you comply to prove your innocence.

This is unacceptable and is abuse. Controlling the victims' banking, not allowing their own accounts, or having to ask permission to spend your own money is abuse. If they cancel appointments without your knowledge and say others cancelled them, that is abuse. Speaking with your work boss and colleagues without you knowing, telling them about your habits, or causing issues with your ability to socialize with them can also be abuse.

TASK

1. Discuss 3 ways of keeping track of someone.

2. When do you believe it is OK to keep track of someone?

3. Discuss 5 methods of controlling another's Money.

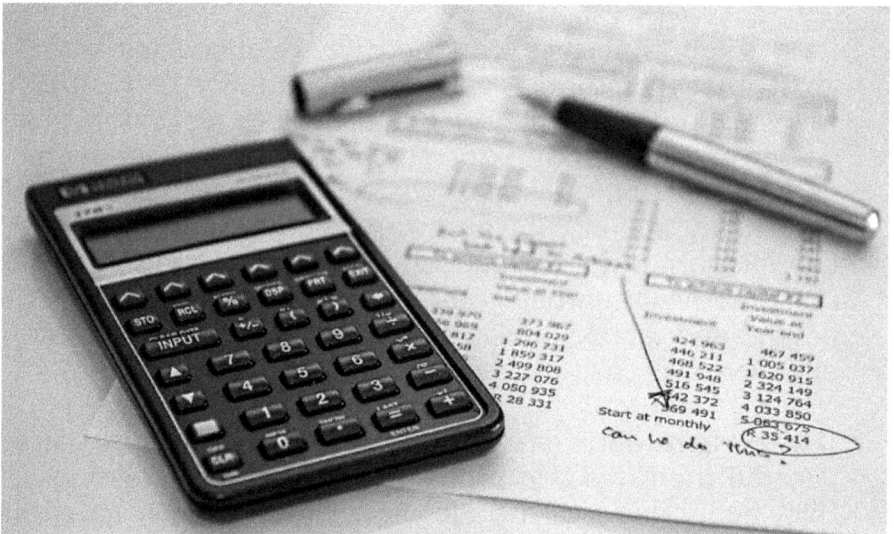

Have you ever been 'ordered' to do something?

Directly ordering you to do something, such as "get my dinner done now", "make me a cup of tea" or "Stop taking the pill" are often expected to be followed without question by the abuser. When you do question them, even if you have plans to the contrary then the rage and abuse can start. Often lasting long after you have given in and just done as you're told. This type of abuse is meant as a punishment, they will often use condescending and patronizing tones almost as if mocking you. They will raise their eyebrows, smirk, or feign disappointment! Abusers do not recognize that you do have the right to refuse, their needs come first and if they don't they brand you selfish. Often you are then treated like a child or end up being on the receiving end of having long conversations about how helpless they are, how much they need and rely on you. They simply cannot live without you.

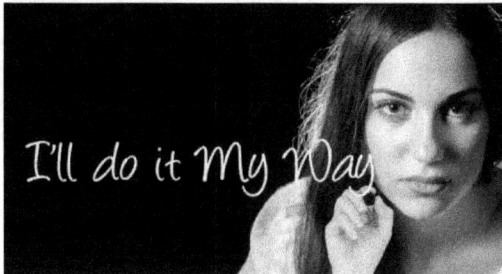

Rages from abusers are a terrible sight to behold, almost unbelievable that a grown adult can act this way! People with personality disorders are very unpredictable and often their rages occur at any time and over small things. These rages have a common connection. Control, power, and shame. It is believed that some people with personality disorders are incapable of feeling more than one strong emotion at a time.

During these rages, every incidence they can think of can be up for debate, even if it occurred last year or 20 years ago. The list of outrageous accusations these types of personalities can accuse you of can actually be a projection of what they can do, or would do if they are in your situation, often using others to help them gain an advantage. Never be fooled into thinking they are 'only joking'. If you have told them you don't like something, it hurts you or upsets you, then it's not a joke and it's become a weapon of choice. To abusers arguments are competitions and they do not like to lose.

Gaslighting.

Gaslighters will blatantly deny they are manipulating the victim, even ignoring evidence even when confronted with it. Gaslighters will not address their bad behavior to the victim, instead, it will always be made to be your fault! You're too 'sensitive' or you're 'crazy'. They simply are unable to put themselves in someone else's shoes. They are the definition of hypocrites, having extremely high morals which their victims must stick to, but they are free to do anything they wish. In relationships where abuse is present, there is often an imbalance of power. You will find yourself apologizing without knowing what you did wrong. Gaslighting is when one person intentionally distorts reality, using lies and misinformation to get their warped reality believed. Victims often question their sanity, perception of reality and memories.

Perpetrators will deceive their victim, consciously most of the time but their actions could be due to a lack of emotional intelligence or understanding. They will systematically chip away at the victim, leaving them feeling confused, anxious, and unable to trust themselves. Gaslighting is a massive subject. Please come back to this as many times as you feel necessary to fully understand its effects and how to protect yourself from this horrendous form of abuse. The recounted excuses will start to seem so familiar to you, the same old promises and actions will never match the promises. It's normal for the victim to find themselves playing detective, even if they have never done so in any other relationship. They are seeking answers to a feeling they can't explain, then blame themselves for being abusive.

"Jane is home alone, she locks the front door and goes upstairs. John returns home, unlocks the front door then starts an argument with Jane for leaving the front door unlocked."

The following are signs and examples of gaslighting, the end result, conscious or not, is to make the other person doubt their own sanity by manipulation of the facts giving the gaslighter the feeling of power and control over their victim. Signs of gaslighting can include;

1. A focus on your own character flaws,
2. Self-esteem is at rock bottom,
3. Second-guessing yourself all the while,
4. You often feel confused,
5. You find it hard or impossible to make decisions,
6. Saying sorry all the while,
7. Feeling like a disappointment,
8. A feeling of disconnection from your past self,
9. Making excuses for the gaslighter's behavior,
10. You lie to yourself to avoid confusion,
11. You believe, or are told you are too sensitive,
12. You are tense around the gas-lighter,

13. You have a sense of something is wrong, but cannot put your finger on it,
14. You feel trapped and cannot see any way out.

Gaslighting is a form of mental and emotional abuse. It promotes anxiety, depression, and can trigger mental breakdowns. Generally victims of gaslighting are depicted as overly emotional, fragile things who can rage and have outbursts at the drop of a hat. Often they are labelled "crazy", this term, which is placed on any individual who expresses their feelings in a passionate way. You don't like certain behaviours – you're crazy. You have your own opinions – you're crazy. As a result, crazy has become a term that others use to get off the hook for their own behaviour. The following are basic examples of gaslighting used by the Narcissist, Sociopath and Psychopath. Remember, these character traits do not just exist in films! They exist in abusers as well!

1. Blatant lying
Characters who use gaslighting tell obvious and lies, unnecessary and even tiny lies. You know that they are lying. The issue is how they are lying with such ease. The gaslighter is setting you up in an abusive pattern. You begin to question everything around you, and become uncertain of the simplest matters and of yourself. This self-doubt is exactly what the gaslighter wants.

2. Deny, Deny, Deny
Again, you know exactly what they have said. However, they completely deny ever saying it. Sometimes victim's go as far as to record the conversations in an attempt to self validate or prove to their abuser that, they are in fact, the abuser! (Legally recordings can be classed as 'abusive' behaviour – further limiting the victims means of gathering evidence) The gaslighter often asks them to 'prove it,' knowing that, in some situations you only have your memory of the conversation. This results in the victim questioning their memory and their reality. Abusers will deny what happened

knowing full well the victim is in the right, from the start they face a losing battle and are further traumatized just attempting to get to the truth! The abuser's enablers (flying monkeys) will back up their side of the story, often because they have been pre-warned about how crazy the victim is, or they simply enjoy the drama and the chance to "get at" the victim. They may even be under the misguided idea they are trying to help you.

3. Using what you love against you
Abusers will often use what is closest to you, against you. If you love your job, they will find issues with it, not enough pay, working around the opposite sex, bad influence, etc. If you have children, the gaslighter may force you to believe you should never have had them, should punish them more, or become jealous of the time you spend with them. This abusive manipulation tactic causes the victim to question the foundation of themselves as well as what they hold close to their heart.

4. The slow death of the victim
One of the terrifying parts of gaslighting is the methodical timeline that the abuser uses. The manipulation happens gradually over time. This has the victim morphing into someone entirely different. The most confident human being can become a shell of a person without even being aware of it. The victim's individual reality disintegrates around them and can result in the victim subconsciously copying the abusive traits of the abuser.

5. Words vs. Actions
Notably, a person who gaslights talks and talks. They can be extremely convincing because they have had a lot of practice! However, their words mean nothing. Therefore, it is important to look at what they are doing. The issues lie in their abusive actions towards the victim.

6. Love and flattery

A common technique of a person who gaslights is to tear you down and then build you back up (the cycle of abuse). The uneasiness the victim feels is because without realizing, they are becoming used to being torn down. However, the praise may lead you to think that the abuser isn't all that bad. The victim often begins to crave this praise which can and does lead to codependency.

7. Confusion

Without a doubt, everyone craves stability. The gaslighter knows this, and the constant confusion that the abuser has instilled leads the victim to become desperate for clarity. More often than not, the victim searches for this clarity in the abuser, trying to heal or help them at first. But finally just trying to make sense of something which cannot be made sense of, thus continuing the cycle of abuse and increasing the power that the abuser has. This confusion often leads to actual memory loss and confusion.

8. Projecting

The abuser's traits of being a liar and a cheater are often hidden apart from those who they abuse. They will believe the victim is capable of the same despicable acts and will accuse you of being the liar and the cheater. You constantly feel like you need to defend yourself for things you haven't done. The abuser will even accuse you of the things they would 'want to' or be 'capable' of doing. Things any normal person could not even get their heads around! In the end the only way to understand an abuser – is to stop understanding them.

9. "You're crazy"

The gaslighter will know you are questioning your sanity. The gaslighter also knows that you come to them trying to make sense of it all, but they are purposefully causing the confusion. So when you are trying to make sense of things, and they call you crazy and the abuser, you might actually believe it.

Furthermore, the gaslighter may tell others such as family, friends, or work colleagues that you're crazy or abusive. This way if you were ever to approach them for help, they wouldn't believe you. This 'heads up' the abuser has given your mutual friends, claiming that this would happen will reinforce the idea that you're too "crazy" to be taken seriously.

10. Everyone else is a liar
The abuser may also instill in you the fear that everyone else is against you and that they are all liars. Again, believing that everyone else is lying or against you forcing your sense of reality to be further blurred. People who gaslight want the power over the victim, that way the victim only has them to turn to for everything. This allows the abuse to continue.

Gaslighting can only be described as a weapon, it aims to degrade someone's mental state making them vulnerable to control or suggestion. The quicker a victim can pick up on these gaslighting techniques, the better luck you will have to avoid the abuse and maintain the distinct reality of your circumstances – this is where a strong support network of family and friends is essential. Not mutual friends, or only the abuser's friends, but having distinct individual friends you can turn to for advice. A strong support network should be encouraged by your partner, not discouraged, which is a red flag. BPD or borderline personality disorder is often diagnosed in cases of abuse as victims will rarely speak out when first seeking help or they are not believed.

Gaslighting is a clear form of psychological abuse and employed by Narcissists, Machiavellians, cult leaders, dictators, and control freaks. We can all resort to a little gaslighting now and again in the hope of swaying another's views or opinions towards our own. Break the Silence has a separate module dedicated to this type of abuse.

The dark triad – the dark side of personality disorders.

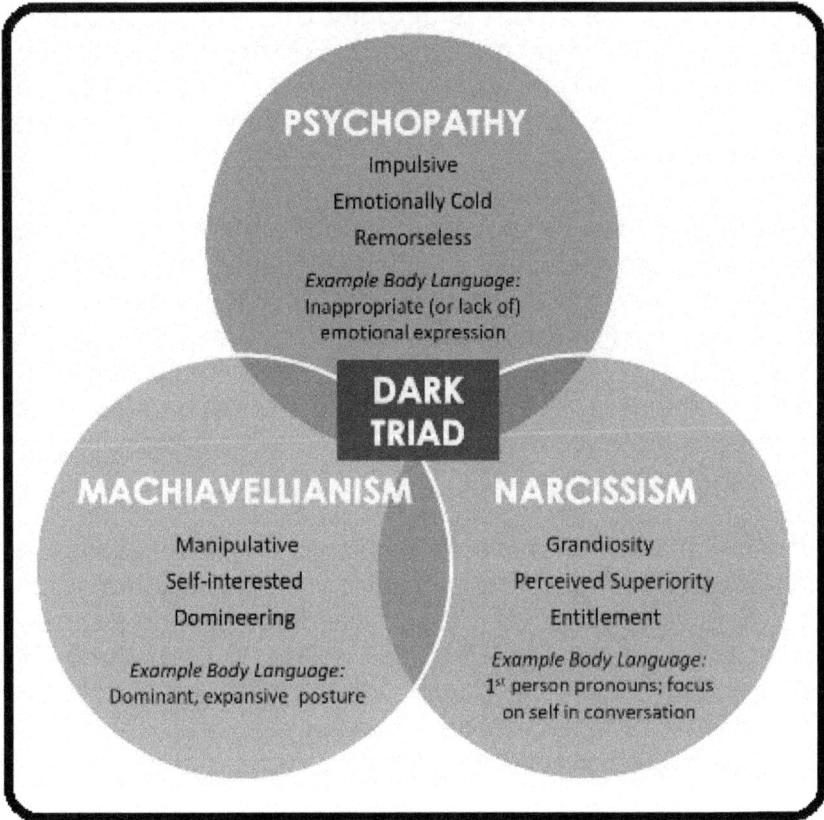

PSYCHOPATHY
Impulsive
Emotionally Cold
Remorseless

Example Body Language:
Inappropriate (or lack of)
emotional expression

**DARK
TRIAD**

MACHIAVELLIANISM
Manipulative
Self-interested
Domineering

Example Body Language:
Dominant, expansive posture

NARCISSISM
Grandiosity
Perceived Superiority
Entitlement

Example Body Language:
1st person pronouns; focus
on self in conversation

Image: theunityprocess.com

Reactive abuse.

Reactive abuse is when a victim reacts to a perpetrator's abuse. The victim may scream, swear, lash out physically or actually start to copy the behavior of the abuser. The abuser then tells the victim and others that they are, in fact, the abuser. Abusers rely on "reactive abuse" because it is their "proof" that the victim is actually the abuser, and not them. Abusers will keep bringing up these reactions in every argument. Reactive abuse is often used to justify going to the police or even filing for injunctions or non-molestation orders of their own.

Reactive abuse is not the same as mutual abuse. Both partners can be equally abusive to one another and many survivors often ask themselves if they are abusive too, because of how they react. www.domesticshelters.org says that mutual abuse is very rare and many experts don't believe it exists. The power and control dynamics involved in domestic violence would make it nearly impossible for both partners to be abusive.

When domestic violence is present, there is always one who initiates or instigates the problems in the relationship. Again it amounts to that one person needing the power and control over their victim. That's what abuse is – the imbalance of power. Don't believe anyone when they say, "Well, we were abusive to each other." Abusers will never accept responsibility for their actions and instead shift blame for the abuse onto others. They often say their behavior is actually because of you being so needy or "a pain", that they are reacting to your abuse. Denying things (gaslighting) you know are real, and using guilt are common in an attempt to get their way. Have you ever been told you owe them something, and to look at all they have done for you? Abusers know which buttons to push, they have been carefully monitoring you for a long time. They know how to upset you and once trouble does start, it's your fault for creating it.

Abusers also have very short memories, denying their abuse to you and others, almost bewildered at the very thought of such bad behavior. It's you, you have anger issues, you have control issues and they are the poor helpless victims. You will find talking about your feelings very hard with abusers because they will accuse you of overreacting and making mountains out of molehills, trivializing you. It's a very difficult situation and often very hard to prove because of how covertly the perpetrators' abuse has been carried out.

Also trying to explain to an abuser that your reactions are because of their actions is impossible. You will find yourself explaining all the basic emotions and feelings that a 3-year-old should know. Even being 'nice' must be explained and they seem to simply have no concept of basic human interaction. Victims will think to themselves, 'if' I can just get them to understand why I'm so hurt, then they'll stop doing it. But they won't stop. They will pretend to be decent human beings, even showing complete understanding in front of others, but in reality, they would not have done these things in the first place if they were. Abusers will accuse the victim of feeling emotions they are intentionally provoking. It's normal to feel jealous if they are blatantly flirting with someone else, especially an ex! This is often over social media, using these other supplies as backups and making themselves feel empowered. At what point does it become acceptable to ask to check their messages, or ask them to prove they are not doing something wrong?

It's highly likely the victim was once an exceptionally easy-going individual. But when someone uses these methods to intentionally provoke reactions, either in private or public to prove how 'hysterical' you are to others, it will turn the victim's outlook and moods upside down. This confusion is temporary and actively researching and taking time for healing after an encounter with an abuser is needed.

It's important to remind the victim that it's common for them to be among the few who see abusers' true colors. Abusers will surround themselves with a fan club of superficial friends.

TASK

1. Think of one of your close friends, what could you say to provoke a reaction?

2. What reaction do you think you could provoke?

3. Now, how could you get them to believe they have overreacted or taken you out of context.

4. Repeat 1-3 for another 2 people.

EVEN GOOD PEOPLE HAVE THEIR LIMITS.

Projection & Triangulation

Psychological projection

From Wikipedia, the free encyclopedia

Psychological projection is a defense mechanism in which the ego defends itself against unconscious impulses or qualities (both positive and negative) by denying their existence in themselves and attributing them to others.[1] For example, a bully may project his or her own feelings of vulnerability onto the target, or a person who is confused may project feelings of confusion and inadequacy onto other people.

Projection incorporates blame shifting and can manifest as **shame dumping**.[2]

Projection has been described as an early phase of introjection.[3]

We all naturally use projection, it is human nature. For instance, if you're in a great mood, but your friend isn't. You continue to smile and maintain your positive mood, projecting it onto your friend. Or, another form of projection could be if your partner is in a bad mood, sees that you're smiling and happy, and they start yelling at you for being cheerful. Your partner is then projecting their mood onto you. Projection is a form of control and manipulation, gaslighting is a common term used to describe someone who is being manipulated by psychological means into doubting their own sanity. Abusers simply can't allow others to be independent because it challenges them, makes life inconvenient, and uncomfortable, so they do everything they can to gain power and control over their victim. Often abusers will live in fantasy worlds where they refuse to see their own faults or acknowledge their failures, which means the blame that would usually be placed on them is projected onto their victims, preventing any type of learning. Abusers can and often are linked to psychopathic traits and narcissism. The same as psychopaths, abusers have little or no shame unless their image is at risk. They can and do goad by continuously criticizing, humiliating and degrading.

In projection, the victim's own opinions and feelings are picked away until their self image and self confidence are destroyed. Abusers can become easily bored so surround themselves with other people who are stimulating and praising them. Often they become quickly uninterested by anything that does not have a positive or thrilling result for them directly, using others as tools to 'get at' the victim. This 'triangulation' can make you feel confused, giving the impression that they are in high demand by their friends all the while. The purpose of this manipulation tactic is to create chaos and keep the victim off balance. Perpetrators using this technique will pit victims against each other for their approval. Flirting with others, inventing stories such as others are flirting with them or the victims friends don't really like them. At first they will seem exciting and all knowing, often making the victim feel quite inferior. Remember... Insecure people are easy to control.

Triangulation (psychology)

WIKIPEDIA
The Free Encyclopedia

From Wikipedia, the free encyclopedia

Triangulation is a manipulation tactic where one person will not communicate directly with another person, instead using a third person to relay communication to the second, thus forming a triangle. It also refers to a form of splitting in which one person manipulates a relationship between two parties by controlling communication between them.

Triangulation may manifest itself as a manipulative device to engineer rivalry between two people, known as divide and conquer[1] or **playing one (person) against another**.[2]

They will accuse you of having anger and control issues. Often playing the victim to your friends and family when you react to their triangulation tactics. Abusers will blame you for all their woes, you never helped them, you're not supportive or you keep interfering in things. All this leads again to the victim accepting the abusive behaviour through fear, guilt or a lack of their own self worth – believing they 'deserve' the abuse.

Personal jokes are often used to attack the personality and character of the victim, again undermining confidence. This is often done as revenge for something they believe you have done to them. They will say you have no sense of humor or tell you to lighten up when you get offended. It is unfortunately also very possible that your abuser will destroy your things, especially personal items that mean a lot. They might crack or destroy your phone or 'lose' your bank card or car keys, then deny it. In long-term or severe cases of domestic abuse, the victims' identity can be destroyed and never recovered. They then need to begin the healing and rebuilding of who they are from the bottom up. It is very important at this point to include a good understanding of abuse, boundaries and the drug-like effect abuse can have to prevent another abusive relationship.

TASK

1. Can you name 3 personality traits of an abuser that they would want to project onto their victim?

2. Consider the other person or someone you know. Now, if you wanted to abuse them through triangulation tactics – who would be the third person and what would you feed them?

3. Consider how you would feel if you did this?

4. How do you believe an abuser would feel?

5. Discuss with your partner the differences between 3 and 4.

Triangulation

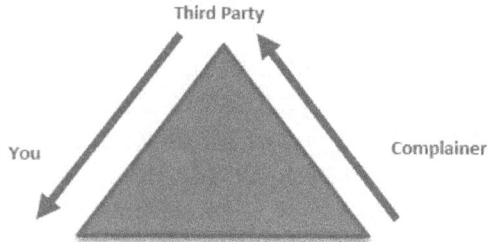

"Narcissists use triangulation to maintain control of family dynamics. The narcissist will pit siblings against each other in order to achieve their goals. The narcissist will lie to one child about the other in order to gain an accomplice in ganging up on their sibling. A narcissist will also lie to both children simultaneously, informing them that they are the favorite child."

Quote: Tina Fuller, Narcissistic Parents

"Toxic people have an incredible ability to triangulate third parties into abusing a victim. This is done on purpose so the toxic person's hands 'stay clean' from the abuse."

Quote: Shannon Thomas, southlakecounseling.org

"Narcissists bring a third person into the mix, many times without that other person knowing. It's also called 'abuse by proxy". Sometimes, the narcissists will even have that third person contact us and 'pass along a message' just to see our reaction. Narcissists want to use another person to abuse us so they can claim innocence. Triangulation is just a way for narcissists to maintain power and control over there targets."

Quote: @FreedomFromNarcissisticAndEmotionalAbuse

Emotional isolation and neglect

'Dehumanizing' is often used by abusers to demand respect. Everything and anything you do wrong, no matter how slight will not go unpunished. You are expected to defer to them on everything, but it's only one-way! If you do try to communicate you are shut down, the subject changed or plain ignored. The victim goes from being showered with non-stop attention and admiration to suddenly feeling isolated and neglected. The abuser seems to have become 'bored' by them. This is when the abuser shows their normal self, the mask slips away and they will become very annoyed that the victim is interested in continuing the passionate relationship that they created in the first place, it's hard work for them. Abusers will manipulate you, or the situation to stop you from socialising, creating drama, distraction or begging you not to go out. They are very good at making the victim believe it's their choice not to go see friends or even not be allowed to leave the house without the abuser. Abusers often cause an argument preventing the victim from even wanting to go out. They may have told family or friends that you don't want to see them, or make excuses why you cannot see them.

Often abusers are telling you one story, others something else. They'll tell co-workers, friends, and the victim's family that they are unstable, argumentative, needy, and abusive. When these misinformed or 'enablers' say something, the victim often chooses to 'keep the peace by not setting the record straight. This becomes the norm and isolation follows. Withholding affection is again very common, they won't touch you or refuse sexual relations and 'closeness' out of spite, to punish you or get you to do something. Victims often feel more alone when with an abuser, unable to communicate out of a fear of their reaction. One massive red flag, one which you should never ignore is indifference. When you're hurt or crying, they do nothing. For example, if you come in after hurting your back and end up collapsing on the floor in pain, crying out, and unable to move. The response you will often get from abusers is "you are an inconvenience", hindrance, or needy. Remember, if it's in front of one of there/your friends or family, the 'act' of the loving caring partner will switch on.

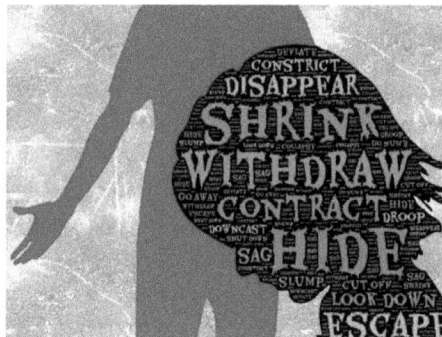

TASK

Discuss how you would feel if you had no-one to turn to, no one who you could just talk about your day or your worries with. If you tried to, you were accused of cheating or being selfish.

Ivory Tower Syndrome

ivory tower noun

Definition of *ivory tower*

1   : an impractical often escapist attitude marked by aloof lack of concern with or interest in practical matters or urgent problems

2   : a secluded place that affords the means of treating practical issues with an impractical often escapist attitude

Credit: merriam-webster.com

Abusers will try to force the victim's image of them, to see the abuser as the centre of the victim's world, almost like an attention seeking child. Interrupting whatever you're doing because they are more important and disputing your feelings. If you're on the phone or texting, they might get in your face and will make it very clear that the attention should be on them, not anyone else. Whatever the victim feels, they will say it's wrong for feeling like that, or that's not how you're actually feeling and they will then try to gaslight you into believing you're actually feeling something else. If you're ill, they will always be worse! If it's your birthday, they will ruin it. Whatever the occasion, be wary of them ruining it and playing the victim or crying wolf to gain the attention they need.

Often how they treat the victims will lead to a discussion about their abusive past, how they are depressed or the trauma they have suffered from a crazy ex (abusers have a lot of crazy ex's). This is often an attempt at making you feel sorry for them, changing the subject and refocusing the discussion. They will attempt to force a bond over their complex emotional state and give you the urge to help or 'fix' them for the better.

Be warned, abusers rarely change, they will cry wolf, sometimes apologize but in the end, they are the wolf! A pattern will soon emerge, apologising will only happen in order for them to gain the upper hand and will not last. In fact, often they will bring this up in further arguments and blame the victim for their actions.

TASK

1. The Ivory Tower is often seen in positions of power, have you ever worked under someone who might have had this condition?
2. Do you know anyone who might have this condition?
3. Discuss how you believe would be best to treat someone like this, remember there is no right or wrong answer.

Codependency

A codependent relationship is when something you do is in reaction to your abuser's behavior (not to be mistaken with reactive abuse). And they need you to boost their own self-esteem. You may have forgotten how to be any other way. It's a vicious circle of unhealthy behavior and imbalance.

You might be codependent if you:

- are unhappy in the relationship, but fear alternatives,
- consistently neglect your own needs for the sake of theirs,
- ditch friends and sideline your family to please your partner,
- frequently seek out your partner's approval,
- criticize yourself through your abuser's eyes,
- ignoring your own instincts,
- make a lot of sacrifices to please the other person, but it's not reciprocated,
- would rather live in the current state of chaos than be alone,
- bite your tongue and repress your feelings to keep the peace,
- feel responsible and take the blame for something they did,

- defend your abuser when others point out what's happening,
- try to "rescue" them from themselves,
- feel guilty when you stand up for yourself,
- think you deserve this treatment,
- believe that nobody else could ever want to be with you,
- change your behavior in response to guilt; your abuser
- says, "I can't live without you," so you stay

There is also a massive selfishness and a thirst for attention from the abuser. Abusers will drain the energy from you, consuming your entire life leaving you exhausted and confused. You will start to seek answers elsewhere, health, fitness, even blaming others for how you feel. At first, you would have been drawn in by the thought that you could fix them or you were the only one who could make them happy. However remember, the truth is: no one can fill the black void of a true abuser's soul! Abusers have so much in common with dark personality disorders, often themselves being hidden psychopaths and narcissists. When the problem is this deep, there is no helping them and you will be left drained and broken while they move onto someone who is unaware of their dark side. No contact is the only real safe route to take.

TASK

1. Discuss with your partner what you believe codependency is,

2. Discuss with your partner the problems of codependency and try and give some examples.

Lying and Excuses

Abusers are very good at manipulation as we have already discussed. They will use any method they can including lying to get the results they want. If that lie is found out, they simply ignore that they have been caught and move on to the next falsehood. They will constantly blame others and spend more time rationalising their behaviour than trying to resolve any conflict. This includes focusing on the mistakes the victim has made, not on their own mistakes in order to throw off the argument. Victims can become confused at the lies being told, often because there is simply not a need for that lie to be told! It's almost as if they want the victim to find them out, craving the drama that is caused. Again, this is where you might be drawn into the circular arguments, explaining the simple values and boundaries of human nature to someone who can be described in no other way, but a brick wall.

One red flag to be aware of personally, is an unusual amount of 'crazy' exes. Anyone who did not come back grovelling on their hands and knees may have been labelled jealous, bipolar, mad or any number of derogatory names. When they do come back, they are held on standby to make the victim jealous or to hook up with if the opportunity presents itself. Make no mistake, the abuser will speak about their current victim in the same way after the discard phase!

Coercive Control

Coercive control – Abusive power and control

From Wikipedia, the free encyclopedia

WIKIPEDIA
The Free Encyclopedia

Abusive power and control (also **controlling behavior** and **coercive control**) is commonly used by an abusive person to gain and maintain power and control over another person in order to subject that victim to psychological, physical, sexual, or financial abuse. The motivations of the abuser are varied and can include devaluation, envy, personal gain, personal gratification, psychological projection, or just for the sake of the enjoyment of exercising power and control.[1]

Controlling abusers use tactics to exert power and control over their victims. The tactics themselves are psychologically and sometimes physically abusive. Control may be exerted through economic abuse, limiting the victim, as they may not have the means to resist or leave the abuse.[2] The goal of the abuser is to control, intimidate, and influence the victim to feel they do not have an equal voice in the relationship.[3]

Manipulators and abusers often control their victims with a range of tactics, including, but not limited to, positive reinforcement (such as praise, superficial charm, flattery, ingratiation, love bombing, smiling, gifts, attention), negative reinforcement (taking away aversive tasks or items), intermittent or partial reinforcement, psychological punishment (such as nagging, silent treatment, swearing, threats, intimidation, emotional blackmail, guilt trips, inattention) and traumatic tactics (such as verbal abuse or explosive anger).[4]

The vulnerabilities of the victim are exploited with those who are particularly vulnerable being most often selected as targets.[4][5][6] Traumatic bonding (also popularly known as Stockholm syndrome) can occur between the abuser and victim as the result of ongoing cycles of abuse in which the intermittent reinforcement of reward and punishment creates powerful emotional bonds that are resistant to change and a climate of fear.[7] An attempt may be made to normalise, legitimise, rationalise, deny, or minimise the abusive behaviour, or blame the victim for it.[8][9][10]

Isolation, gaslighting, mind games, lying, disinformation, propaganda, destabilisation, brainwashing, and divide and rule are other strategies that are often used. The victim may be plied with alcohol or drugs or deprived of sleep to help disorientate them.[11][12] Based on statistical evidence, certain personality disorders correlate with abusive tendencies of individuals with those specific personality disorders when also compiled with abusive childhoods themselves. [13]

The seriousness of coercive control in modern Western societies has been increasingly realised with changes to the law in several countries so it is a definable criminal offence. In conjunction with this there have been increased attempts by the legal establishment to understand the characteristics and effects of coercive control in legal terminology. For example, on January 1, 2019, Ireland enacted the Domestic Violence Act 2018, which allowed for the practice of coercive control to be identifiable based upon its effects on the victim. And on this basis defining it as: 'any evidence of deterioration in the physical, psychological, or emotional welfare of the applicant or a dependent person which is caused directly by fear of the behaviour of the respondent'.[14] On a similar basis of attempting to understand and stop the widespread practice of coercive control, in 2019, the UK government made teaching about what coercive control was a mandatory part of the education syllabus on relationships.[15] While coercive control is often considered in the context of an existing intimate relationship, when it is used to elicit a sexual encounter it is legally considered as being a constituent part of sexual abuse or rape. When it is used to begin and maintain a longer term intimate relationship it is considered to be a constituent element of sexual slavery.

Coercive control is when an abuser repeatedly does something in a way that makes their victim feel isolated, controlled, dependent, or scared. Often saying they'll harm the victim, themselves, pets, or family members.

These types of behavior are common examples of coercive control as well as using both physical and emotional abuse as described earlier, this list is by no means exhaustive, how many have happened to you?

- Isolating the victim from friends and family,
- Controlling someone's money,
- Monitoring a person's movements and activities,
- Repeatedly putting someone down, calling them names, or telling them they're worthless,
- Threatening to harm someone or their children or pets,
- Threatening to publish private information about someone,
- Falsely reporting someone to the police,
- Damaging goods or property,
- Forcing someone to take part in criminal activity or child abuse,
- Gaslighting,
- Reinforcing the roles within a relationship,
- Manipulating others (flying monkeys) or engaging in parental alienation,
- Controlling what you wear, how you look, how often you wash and what essentials you can use,
- Sexual coercion, using sex to control you or get what they want.

Some of these behaviors can also be other offenses as well as coercive control. So a perpetrator can be arrested for more than one offense, for the same behavior. For example, if a perpetrator broke a phone as part of their coercive control then they could be arrested and charged for coercive control and also the offense of criminal damage. An abuser damages the victim's possessions but rarely their own property or the property of others in the household, again showing a deliberate action and not of a loss of self-control. An abuser will only be guilty of the offense of coercive control if their behavior has had a serious effect on the person and that he/she knew or ought to have known that their behavior would have a serious effect on that person. It is also very common for abusers to use those you love to further control you, often children or pets. Abusers can threaten to harm, kidnap, or even claim they will 'take the children from them'. Abusers will also use guilt, saying the victim is breaking up the family. Remembering that Children do have a voice is very important and speaking with them away from any influencing party is routinely practiced by professionals to gain a more accurate and 'bigger picture.

TASK

1. Do you believe that you have ever been a victim of this type of abuse?

2. Looking at yourself, have you ever done or been tempted to coerce others using the methods above?

3. Discuss how the intelligence of an abuser affects his/her ability to understand how coercive abuse affects the victim.

4. What changes do you think should be made to help combat coercive control.

5.

Social Abuse

Social abuse is humiliation, this cruel treatment includes public threats, intimidation, and gossip. As well as joking at your expense, constant heckling or teasing to provoke a response to then project the blame onto you. It also includes tickling, touching, kissing, or other forms of physical acts that you have asked your partner to refrain from in public – this is entirely dependent on your, your feelings, and what you have asked them not to do. Any behavior designed to upset you in front of others is social abuse.

Some examples of Social Abuse;

- Refuses to socialize with your family or friends,
- Encourages friends who are abusive,
- Demands you move away from friends and a supportive environment.
- Monitors your social activities,
- Alienates you from your family and friends,
- Treats you disrespectfully in front of others,
- Tells secrets or embarrassing stories about you,
- Refuses to let you work outside the home,
- Demands that you account for all your time with social contacts,
- Controls who you can visit and when,
- Gossips or spread rumors about you.

It's expected that most of the above are practiced by an abuser as part of the abusive relationship.

The disclosure of confidential information or embarrassing events to co-workers and friends is also classed as socially abusive behaviour. Gossiping, spreading rumors, and playing mind games or gaslighting are effective means of controlling others.

So is using social media. Abusers can be masters at tearing up and looking 'ever-so-sincere' before disclosing embarrassing information about their victim in the form of "sharing concerns" and "advice". The only true-fire way of fighting these games is not to play. Do not waste your time outwitting the abuser, every time you clear up one issue, another two have popped up. Going no contact is the hardest thing in the world (especially if you care for them still, which is often the case in abusive relationships due to the trauma bonding effect). It is the most rewarding and only truly safe path to take with abusers. It is also very common that when a victim leaves an abusive relationship and the abuser can no longer control them directly, they will try and control how others see them. The misinformation will feel unfair and often leads to professionals getting involved such as police, social services, and other safeguarding parties especially if there are children involved. Staying above it, and trusting that eventually others will see the truth is the only way to avoid the mental damage this abuse can do. By distancing yourself or going 'grey rock' the survivor is able to maintain some sense of self and prevents them from falling into the trap the abuser sets for them, namely, provoking them in front of others to make them appear guilty.

The grey rock method involves communicating in an uninteresting way when interacting with abusive or manipulative people. The name "grey rock" refers to how those using this approach become unresponsive, similar to a rock.

The technique may involve:

- avoiding interactions with the abusive person
- keeping unavoidable interactions brief
- giving short or one-word answers to questions
- communicating in a factual, unemotional way

The aim is to cause the abusive person to lose interest and stop their antagonistic behavior, to protect a person's emotional well-being.

Credit: medicalnewstoday.com

I also want to bring attention to the 'privilege' in this section, where the perpetrator defines their role in the relationship (Ivory Tower). For instance, the traditional definition of male and female roles, the female must not question her man's needs, desires or actions. Abusers will often dominate and make all the important decisions, directly or through manipulation of the victim.

TASKS

You suspect that someone close to you is attempting to socially isolate you.

1. Name three ways they could be doing this?
2. Discuss the 'traditions' you feel could be classed as abuse today.
3. Discuss the differences between no contact and grey rock, making sure to include the reasons why you would choose one over the other.

Sexual Abuse

Sexual abuse, is abusive sexual behaviour by one person upon another. This includes rape and sexual assault. This type of abuse can have ongoing physical and emotional effects. Professional counselling is often needed.

Victims can be reluctant to discuss or report sexual abuse. The British Crime Survey indicates that in cases of serious sexual assault, the rapist is actually more likely to be a current or ex-partner, or known to the victim (89% of female and 83% of male victims), with only a minority of rapes being committed by strangers. Sexual abuse can include the use of force, threats, manipulation, drugs, sleeping or intimidation. These are often used to make another person perform sexual acts or coerce them into having sex when they do not want to. It may include forcing the victim to use pornography or have sex with other people.

Sexual abuse also includes behaviour which degrades a person's sexuality. The 'home office 2001a' report found that 53% of homophobic abuse reported to the police happens in the home in contrast to 17% on the street.

If you suspect anyone of sexual abuse, please report it to the police. Sarah's law is a method for you to check your partner for offenses relating to child sexual abuse if you suspect anything. Any offenses disclosed during a request for Sarah's law will be dealt with in the same way as reporting a crime directly to the police.

All rape and sexual assaults are serious but the terms rape and 'sexual assault' are used simply to differentiate between two types of offense.

- Rape is when a male intentionally penetrates another's vagina, anus, or mouth with a penis, without the other person's consent.
- Assault by penetration is when a person penetrates another person's vagina or anus with any part of the body other than a penis, or by using an object, without the person's consent.

The definition overall of 'sexual' or 'indecent' assault is simply an act of physical, psychological and emotional violation in the form of a sexual act, inflicted on someone without their consent. Not all cases of sexual assault involve violence, cause physical injury or leave visible marks. Sexual assault can cause severe distress, emotional harm and injuries which can't be seen – all of which can take a long time to recover from.

The following are examples of sexual abuse:

- Insisting on anything sexual that frightens or hurts you,
- Withholding sex as a form of control,
- Demanding sex/Forcing sex,
- Name-calling with sexual epithets,
- Demanding sex after a violent incident,

- Alleging that you have a history of prostitution on legal papers,
- Forcing you to engage in prostitution or pornography,
- Forcing you to have sex with others besides your partner,
- Unwanted touching,
- Refusing to use safe sex practices,
- Controlling your decisions about pregnancy and/or abortion,
- Videotaping or photographing sexual acts and posting the footage without your permission,
- Preventing you from using birth control.

TASK

Jane and John are divorcing but go on a pre-planned holiday that was booked before they separated. John is asleep and under medication which makes it difficult for him to wake up. Jane initiated sex while John was still asleep, it takes time for him to wake up so by the time he realizes what has happened, they have had full sex. John feels dirty and never consented to this action.

1. Discuss the above example, is this rape, or sexual assault?
2. Discuss the differences between rape and sexual assault?
3. Can you imagine an example like above that would be classed as sexual abuse?
4. What separates sex, or a gesture of affection, from sexual assault?

Financial/Economic Abuse

Economic or financial abuse can start subtle and is often very hard to detect, often financial abuse is intended to make it financially impossible for the victim to leave or have a life outside of the relationship. Abusers have a lack of understanding or lack of regard for others' boundaries and rights to their own money. Often they will take or misuse someone else's money or belongings for their own gain.

An example is;

A man's brother is mentally challenged and has his benefits going into a post office account. His brother and sister who jointly care for him, seeing the amount of money in this account believe they have a right to this money simply because the mentally incapable brother does not have the capacity to understand the value of money and does not 'need' that amount. This results in the capable siblings stealing money from his account in order to buy a new car or holidays.

Financial abuse can be anything to do with money, property, or belongings. It can often be pushed under the carpet and forgotten just to keep the peace. The effects of such abuse on the victim can be very harmful and not just deprive the victim but disadvantage them in areas, further leading to the thoughts they are incapable of looking after themselves. It's important to remember that financial abuse doesn't always involve a crime like theft or fraud. Examples of financial abuse;

- Borrowing money and/or not giving it back,
- Stealing the victim's belongings,
- Taking the victims wages, pension, or other types of
- income,

- Taking or asking for money as payment for normal things couples or friends do, such as visiting or spending time together,
- Forcing or manipulating the victim to sell their home,
- Stealing or holding bank cards, details, etc,
- Forcing or manipulating changes in wills, property, or inheritance,
- Unexplained money loss which cannot be explained,
- No money to pay for essentials such as rent, bills, and food, often having to ask or beg for essentials,
- Refused access to check their own bank accounts or balance,
- Changes in the standards of living i.e. not having items or things they would usually have or need such as grooming items or clothing,
- Unusual or inappropriate purchases in bank statements,
- Using inappropriate powers such as the power of attorney to access another person's money without their consent.

Again this list is not inclusive of every type of financial abuse. Financial abuse can be committed by anyone anywhere, even people employed to provide care. Spouses, friends, family, and neighbours are all capable as well as volunteers, even strangers. Financial abuse can affect anyone but often takes place where there is an unequal balance of power. These are often victims of another form of abuse such as domestic abuse or violence, individuals with learning disabilities or medical conditions where strong medication is needed are especially vulnerable.

Dating Abuse

Dating Violence Occurs in Different Ways

Physical	Emotional	Sexual	Stalking
Pinching	Threatening	Forcing a	A pattern
Spitting	Name-Calling	partner	of
Shoving	Gaslighting	into a	unwanted,
Kicking	Character-	sexual act	harrassing
Punching	Assassination	when they	or threating
Pushing	Minimisation	cannot or	behaviour
Slapping	Isolation	does not	that causes
Burning	Neglect	consent	fear
	Lying		

"What is Abuse" by Stephen Cooke

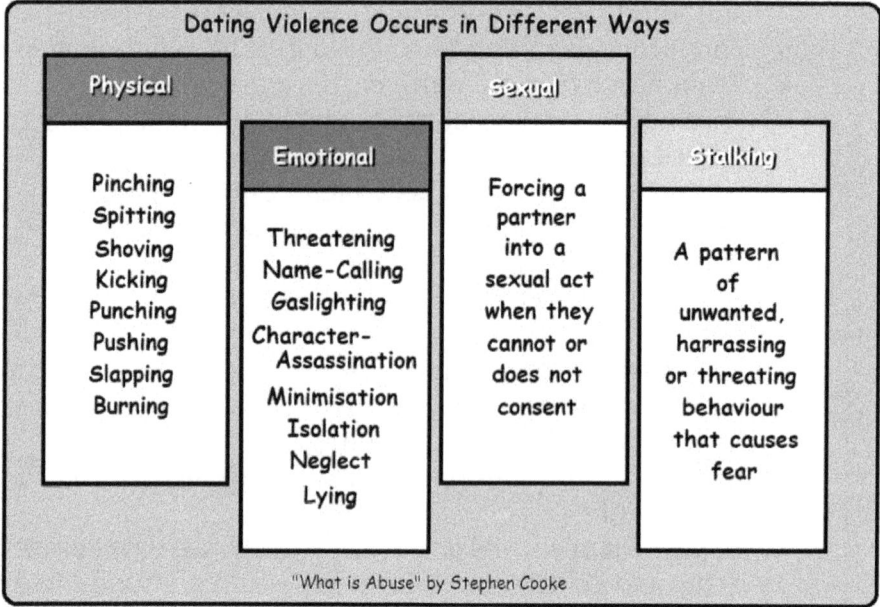

Dating abuse is the term given to abuse while two partners are intimately dating, more often to those under the age of 25. Surveys conducted by the NSPCC and End Violence Against Women campaign show that approximately 40% of young people experience abuse in their teens. The surveys also point out that sexual violence is higher in young people than any other age range with 1-in-5 teenage girls being assaulted at the hands of their boyfriend.

Additional studies have also shown that young people who are subject to abuse are at a higher risk of further violence, riskier sexual behaviour, substance abuse and eating disorders than people who have known healthy relationships.

The differences between healthy and toxic relationships.

Reading and familiarizing yourself with this book will help you recognize the signs of both a healthy relationship and an unhealthy relationship.

The differences between them can be obvious from an outsider, but get very muddled when you experience things yourself.

Characteristics of a Healthy relationship.

Good communication is at the heart of a healthy relationship. Both simple and difficult subjects need to be discussed and problems do arise which need to be talked about and a decision made together. Trust, respect and honesty are signs of a healthy relationship. Could you trust your partner around someone else who liked them, or respect them enough to allow their own boundaries and separate friends? Please see our book "Be Abuse Aware - Boundaries").

It's also important that you enjoy spending time together, and equally enjoy spending time with your own family and friends apart from each other. Seeing both partners as equals and openly discussing relationship problems and sexual choices will allow for a better future.

Behaviors that might indicate abuse.

Some general red flags to watch for are past patterns of abuse, cruelty to animals or children, and hypersensitivity. Abusers can be easily angered and they react aggressively and blow things out of proportion very quickly. They tend to blame everyone but themselves. They often feel someone is out to get them, holding them back, or is not supporting them how they should.

Examples of Verbal and emotional abuse:

1. Name-calling, saying things to others about you, and saying things that make you feel guilty.
2. 'Raging'. Temper tantrums are often used and yelling, screaming, or threatening to hurt themselves or those you care about.
3. Pretending to be concerned about you when really it is control – "don't take that job it's too hard", "don't drive there, it's too dark" etc. – abusers will often start making all their partners decisions from what there wearing, to who they talk to,
4. Putting you down, you look fat, that dress is horrible or what you say or do is always wrong,
5. Jealousy, often mistaken for love is the opposite of trust and accusations of flirting, cheating, or being consistently suspicious,
6. Embarrassing you in public or causing a scene in front of others,
7. Threatening to end the relationship or moving too quickly in order to trap you,
8. Spreading rumors and lies about you to your friends, family, or other people,
9. Blaming you for the abuse or denying that it is happening.

Examples of physical abuse:

- Any action that physically hurts another's body,
- Shoving, Pinching, Scratching, Slapping, Spitting,
- Pushing, Punching, Hitting, Kicking, Hair pulling,
- Strangulation (also during sex, is now classed as abuse under the 2021 Domestic Abuse Act – UK –) or other life-threatening abuse.

Sexual abuse:

- Unwanted harassment, touching, and kissing,
- Forcing you to have sex or perform other sexual acts,
- Manipulating or forcing you to engage in sex acts with others or animals,
- Not allowing you to use birth control or protection.

If you start dating, it's a good idea to give it at least 3-6 months before committing yourself to a relationship. That doesn't mean seeing other people or treating them as an option but keep on your guard, look out for the mask slipping and get to know them before falling head over heels in love.

Risk Factors of Domestic Abuse

There are numerous risk factors that can increase the intensity and frequency of domestic abuse.

Identifying abuse is only the first step, it's now time to get your support network in place. The following is a list of perpetual triggers that increase domestic abuse.

Alcohol misuse. Alcohol consumption itself doesn't cause domestic abuse, but when it is used by an abuser, it will increase the severity and frequency. If the victim is also misusing alcohol, this can increase their susceptibility to abuse.

Age. Younger people are more at risk of abuse simply due to their inexperience than older people. (Walby & Allen 2004).

Ending the relationship. Victims are more at risk of serious abuse after leaving the relationship. Abusers will attempt to use more extreme methods of regaining control and are known to falsely report victims to authorities in order to punish them. Gender.

Gender plays a crucial role in violence and abuse in society. Both males and females can be victims and perpetrators of abuse. Research has shown that the rates of abuse differ significantly between men and women (Stanko 2006, p. 552). This report shows women are significantly more at risk of domestic abuse than men.

Pregnancy. There is a common belief that having a child can bring a couple closer together. This is not true and evidence has suggested that abuse can often start during pregnancy (30% of DV starts during pregnancy – British Medical Association 1998).

A victims 'cycle of abusive partners'. Often victims are so used to being controlled and in a world full of drama they will seek out a similar partner in the future to fill this 'void' they perceive in themselves. Often this will lead to avoiding real nurturing relationships or 'good' partners because they find them boring. This cycle is often associated with drug dependency for an example of how the victim can feel about future partners and their need for this type of partner. Remaining single in order to heal is so important here because the victim needs to re-adjust their boundaries and self-confidence so they can be happy in a future relationship. This should not be confused with the Cycle of abuse/Violence theory developed by Lenore Walker in 1979, The battered woman. This theory is used to explain the cycle of abuse within a single relationship only.

Illness and Unemployment. Illness and unemployment will add to the stress of a person, building on the 'tension-building' stage of abuse. Often this coincides with financial or legal issues. Illness can also be seen by an abuser as another form of control over their victim. Playing on another's vulnerability to subjugate their self-esteem and confidence further.

TASK

Can you answer these?

1. Does the definition of domestic abuse describe when a man is violent to a woman when a woman is violent to a man or something else? Please discuss with your volunteer or partner if it's something else.

2. Nobody is perfect, many of these abusive traits you, or others you know could use without even knowing! Can you name two things you do that could be considered abusive?

3. Domestic abuse increases when you leave a relationship, there are many different reasons for this, can you name 3?

4. When a victim leaves an abusive relationship it's like coming off a drug, they crave that type of relationship again which is why often they enter another abusive relationship. What steps can you take to stop this from happening?

5. Does domestic abuse stop when a woman becomes pregnant?

RISK FACTORS

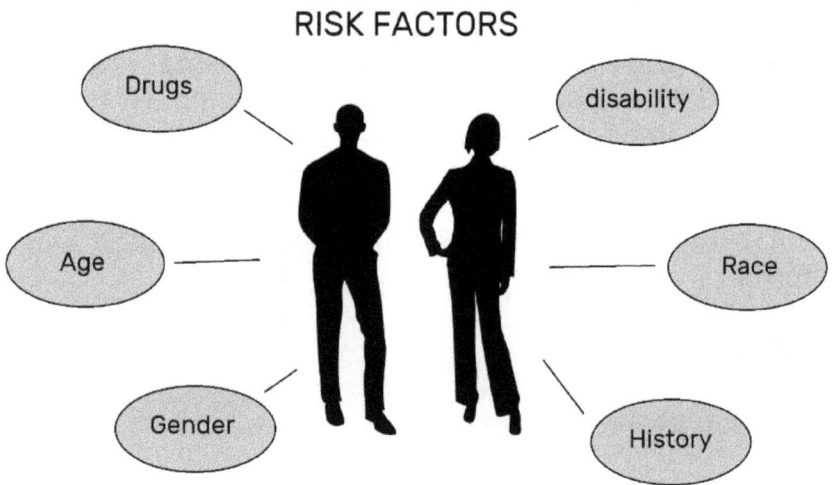

Drugs

disability

Age

Race

Gender

History

Parental Alienation

Parental alienation is complex and there is no single definition. CAFCASS recognizes parental alienation as "when a child's resistance or hostility towards one parent is not justified and is the result of psychological manipulation by the other parent."

With this type of abuse, it's important that all other risk factors such as domestic abuse are resolved first to allow for children to be safe. Children can reject the other parent or resist spending time with them because of the alienating behaviors of the other parent. This type of abuse does have a varying impact on individual children depending on the child's resilience and vulnerability. Alienation can occur quite openly such as a parent constantly badmouthing the other parent, physically stopping contact, forbidding discussion about them, and creating the impression in the child's mind that the other parent dislikes or does not love the child.

Tactics used can also be quite insidious such as talking about their experiences as a child and saying you (the child) are too young to understand what your own eyes are telling you and will understand as you get older, this is also gaslighting and a dangerous manipulation technique.

Isolating children from their support network, terrorizing them, and denying them their emotional needs. Parents who alienate create a false belief that the other parent is dangerous or unworthy.

Limited examples;

1. Talking about their own experiences or third party lives to influence your relationships with either parent,
2. Taking over the conversations when trying to talk about something that happened so they don't have to admit responsibility and 'look bad',
3. Attempting to manipulate the situation using gaslighting or other methods to see things from their point of view,
4. Saying that the 'details' are not important when they are explaining their version of the truth,
5. Justifying the actions of themselves or another that has been witnessed by putting the blame onto someone else, normally the alienated parent,
6. Lies or says a half-truth so that you start to question the other parent,
7. Using phrases such as 'I'm going, to be honest, you are old enough now, do you know what your …. did?"
8. Saying how the alienated parent hurt them, caused them pain, and damaged them so you sympathize with their side,
9. Showering the child with gifts and saying the other parent doesn't care enough to do this, or criticizes the other parent saying they don't treat them,
10. Saying things like "there is no bad blood between us" or "we will always put you, children, first" then proceeding to say the other parent is a liar,
11. Saying they miss and love the children and hate not seeing them more making out the other parent is stopping them from seeing the children,
12. Making jokes between comments about the other parent to curtail the conversation away from what they have just said and preventing confronting or denying the 'said' comments,
13. Saying they love you more than the other parent,
14. Not accepting responsibility even when they know what they have done.

Remember that phrase "in the child's best interests."

The effect of alienation on children can be lifelong. Their sense of identity, self-esteem, and confidence as well as their morals and beliefs can all be negatively affected by such actions. Post-separation, regularly assessing your own behaviour and the best interests of the child is very important, especially if there are strong negative emotions to the other parent.

Health and well-being

The impacts of domestic abuse on anyone cannot be understated, leading to depression, anxiety, aggression, trauma-related symptoms, self-harm, eating disorders, substance abuse, and C-PTSD. The effects are diverse, long-lasting, and debilitating, including detriments to physical and mental health, increased rates of suicide and self-harm, increased alcohol and drug misuse, as well as rises in the likelihood of being unemployed and becoming homeless. In most cases, the basis of abuse lies in socio-cultural norms such as dowry, child marriage, a need for control, personality disorders, and normalization or inherited views of violence against women. Any form of abuse can cause or lead to serious physical and psychological effects. In my own personal experience of abuse, because of my old school values and 'sticking' it out for 25 years, my memory and concentration was massively affected, even now I still suffer 'mind drops' where I return to this state of numbness and memory loss which affects my daily living. Victims of domestic violence do suffer many mixed emotions such as fear, confusion, anger, numbness, guilt, and shame. Many victims do try to cover up the visible effects of violence with makeup or covering the bruises or scratches with clothes. Getting help for abuse in a timely manner can help prevent the long-term impact of abuse on your mental health. If you believe you are suffering from abuse, and start noticing your memory is suffering, you have word-finding difficulty, or are forgetting simple things see your GP in private and explain your concerns. The usual route in the UK is to refer you for help if you agree, and GP's can also refer you to the secondary mental health service. Your mental health can then be assessed and treated. This also opens up many avenues for additional help, such as a domestic abuse support worker. Please use these services, they are not there to penalize or mistreat you, they are there to help so be open with them.

The most obvious impact of domestic abuse is physical injury, it has been recorded that 70% of domestic abuse injuries to the victim are physical, domestic abuse was also linked to a number of health problems in the Crisp & Stanko 2001 study, including sexually transmitted infections (STD's), unwanted pregnancies, irritable bowel syndrome, and gynecological problems. Abuse, in general, is the most prevalent cause of depression and mental health difficulties in women. This can and often does lead to victims self-harming and/or attempting suicide. In a study in 1996 by Stark & Flitcraft, 33% of women attending accident and emergencies for self-harm had experienced domestic abuse and it was noted that women who have experienced domestic abuse are five times more likely to attempt suicide. Both genders can and do suffer abuse. Current trends and surveys show that men are more likely to commit abuse against women, and women are more likely to report this abuse.

Survivors of domestic abuse could have been in toxic relationships for years or decades without actually realizing it. They are often diagnosed with a 'generalized anxiety disorder' or/and depression and trauma. These are serious mental health disorders and the symptoms are very broad and different for everyone.

Claire's law

It's perfectly normal to want to know more when you're buying a new house or new car, after all they are VERY important objects in your life and you wouldn't just take the past owner's words on their condition! You would look into their past and possibly even pay a third-party specialist for their evaluation. These laws cannot be used as a form of control or harassment as the Police carry out their own risk assessments and alongside other safeguarding agencies, will consider whether any information disclosure is legal, necessary, and proportionate. Remember only 23% to 35% of domestic abuse is reported and only around 5% of these lead to convictions. It's better to be safe, not sorry. Why then are some so scared to look into the past of a new partner, especially when things are starting to get serious and you're considering the next steps. There are ways to do this, for both domestic abuse and in relation to safeguarding your children. Everyone has bad traits and red flags will pop up from time to time, if you or a friend gets concerned you can do one of two things. Ask them outright, or look into their past. With both of the following, you will need their names, date of birth, previous names, address, and previous addresses if known. Please understand any disclosure is normally in person at a police station or at your home. If they do have a record, you will be given information to enable you to make an informed choice of your future together. If they have no record then the request could be stopped at any time by the police and you would be informed. The Domestic Violence Disclosure Scheme is known as 'Clare's Law' in the UK, an initiative named after 36-year-old Clare Wood who was murdered by her boyfriend in 2009. Its aim is to protect people from domestic abuse. You have the right to ask the police whether a current partner represents a risk of violence. Others such as concerned third parties, parents, friends, etc can also apply. If the police have information that may impact the safety of that person they will inform them. Normally this process should take around 15-35 days.

If there are serious concerns or a crime has been reported during the reporting process then the police will act quickly. If just information is needed because you have been with an abuser in the past then asking these questions should NOT be an issue to your partner. If they get angry and start to threaten you, make you 'feel' bad for not trusting them, then that is cause to worry and even more cause for checking them out. You can start a Claire's Law by contacting the police (United Kingdom). They will ask your reasons and if any crime has been committed as well as if the person you are asking about knows you are asking for this information and how they might react if they find out.

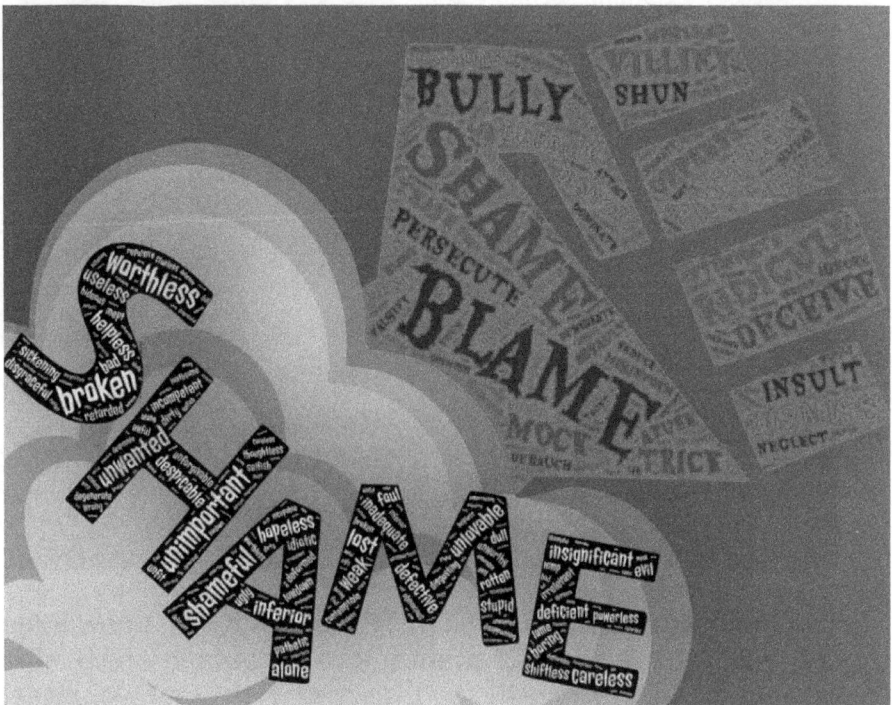

"You are never obliged to accept abuse from anyone, friends, family, or partner."

Sarah's Law

This is another type of disclosure program but aimed towards child sex offenses. If your new partner is going to have access to your children and you have concerns, this law allows anyone to formally ask the police if they have any child sexual offenses. Some police authorities have online forms you can fill in, otherwise, you can ring 101 and ask them to make a request under Sarah's law. Normally the information is only given to a parent or carer and any information given must be kept confidential as legal action could be taken if the information is disclosed to anyone else.

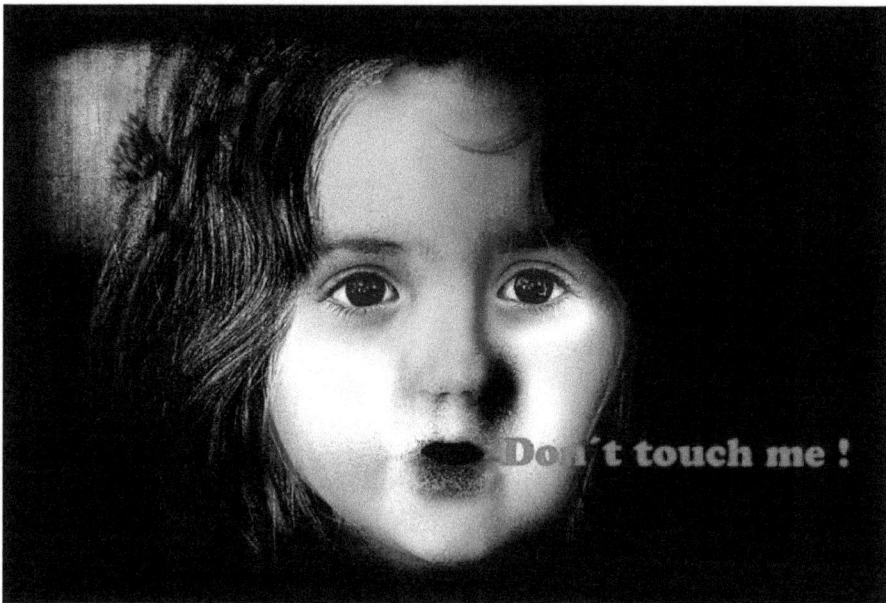

Don't touch me !

The following sections will give you a basic knowledge of recognizing the signs of mental and emotional abuse. Please take each section slowly and discuss with your volunteer or support worker. Remember Abuse is a scale, it's important to talk through your experiences with a professional to fully understand abuse.

Negative Reinforcement

Negative reinforcement in this concept (used by an abuser) simply uses verbal reassurances, manipulation, or lies to strengthen (reinforce) the idea or outcome the perpetrator wants and in doing so, convinces you that their way is the best or only way to avoid a negative outcome (Aversive Stimuli).

Aversive Stimuli

WIKIPEDIA
The Free Encyclopedia

From Wikipedia, the free encyclopedia

In psychology, aversives are unpleasant stimuli that induce changes in behavior via negative reinforcement or positive punishment. By applying an aversive immediately before or after a behavior the likelihood of the target behavior occurring in the future is reduced. Aversives can vary from being slightly unpleasant or irritating to physically, psychologically and/or emotionally damaging. It is not the level of unpleasantness or intention that matter, but rather the level of effectiveness the unpleasant event has on changing (decreasing) behavior that defines something as aversive.

Abusers can expertly reinforce beliefs and convince you that some type of discomfort, either physical or psychological will be avoided by following their idea. If you follow their instructions you will avoid the nasty consequences.

The type of influence an abuser has can be quite difficult to expose. Examples can be a great way to get a better idea of how someone can influence your beliefs.

Consider the following examples:

- In order to avoid sunburn, you are told to use sunscreen,
- You make a mess and are told to clean it up to avoid an argument,
- You leave the house early to avoid getting stuck in traffic and being late for work,
- Someone is a terrible cook, but are constantly telling you how good they are and how good there food tastes,

All these examples avoid negative outcomes by influencing you into performing a specific behavior or action. Most are good but abusers use the same tactics to convince you to do things or think things their way, rather than distorting the truth as in gaslighting (Page 39).

One of the best ways to understand this behavior is to think of it as something being subtracted from the situation to give a better outcome for the abuser, not yourself.

Examples of reinforcing influence in abuse;

- Telling you how you need to give the abuser money to 'prevent' something bad from happening,
- Telling you to behave in a certain way in front of others to prevent them from not liking you,
- Telling you to hurt someone or attack someone to teach them a lesson and respect you,
- Shifting a negative focus away from them to you - such as if the police want to question the abuser but they instead tell you to lie for them or you will be in trouble instead or lose your children, the house or your family,
- Someone new wants to be your friend or help you, but your partner doesn't like them so consistently tells you how bad they are, using methods such as your always upset around them, they are planning something bad, only after your money, trying to steal you away from them,
- They constantly tell you that you are controlling, but are themselves monitoring your whereabouts and phone at all times,
- They keep telling you they care for you and you should not be out late - but in reality they like to control you and are using this as an excuse. The constant talk about it is reinforcing that belief.

Quotes for reflection

"I was afraid to have knives in the house, I knew when she was in a temper, there would be no second-guessing and no remorse afterward! I knew I would simply be gone"
– Anonymous

"do not look for healing at the feet of those who broke you"
— Rupi Kaur, Milk, and Honey

"Arguments would last for hours or days, often over the smallest thing. A wet cloth on the sink, a slight glance at the opposite sex, or a simple human mistake"
– Anonymous

"Of pain, you could wish only one thing: that it should stop. Nothing in the world was so bad as physical pain. In the face of pain, there are no heroes."
—George Orwell, 1984

"In every single argument, the cause of it was ignored and every single thing I had ever done wrong was bought into it. I found myself apologizing again and again for things I never really understood and I was constantly walking on eggshells afraid to bring up anything which needed discussing in case it ended badly"
– Anonymous

"In order to escape accountability for his crimes, the perpetrator does everything in his power to promote forgetting. If secrecy fails, the perpetrator attacks the credibility of his victim. If he cannot silence her absolutely, he tries to make sure no one listens."
— Judith Lewis Herman, Trauma and Recovery: The Aftermath of Violence – From Domestic Abuse to Political Terror

"Often it isn't the initiating trauma that creates seemingly insurmountable pain, but the lack of support after."
— S. Kelley Harrell, Gift of the Dreamtime - Reader's Companion

"You can recognize survivors of abuse by their courage. When silence is so very inviting, they step forward and share their truth so others know they aren't alone."
— Jeanne McElvaney, Healing Insights: Effects of Abuse for Adults Abused as Children

"Shouldn't there be more distaste in our mouths for the abusers than for those who continue to love the abusers?"
— Colleen Hoover, It Ends with Us

"Nobody has ever killed themselves over a broken arm. But every day, thousands of people kill themselves because of a broken heart. Why? Because emotional pain hurts much worse than physical pain."
— Oliver Markus Malloy, Bad Choices Make Good Stories (Omnibus): How The Great American Opioid Epidemic of The 21st Century Began - a Memoir

"Memories demand attention and these memories will have teeth."
— C. Kennedy, Slaying Isidore's Dragons

"You can recognize survivors by their creativity. In soulful, insightful, gentle, and nurturing creations, they often express the inner beauty they brought out of childhood storms."
— Jeanne McElvaney, Childhood Abuse: Tips to Change Child Abuse Effects

"One of the best ways of repressing emotions is artificial certainty."
— Stefan Molyneux

"It is a rare person who can cut himself off from mediate and immediate relations with others for long spaces of time without undergoing a deterioration in personality."
— Harry Stack Sullivan, The Interpersonal Theory of Psychiatry

"Instead of saying, "I'm damaged, I'm broken, I have trust issues," say "I'm healing, I'm rediscovering myself, I'm starting over."
— Horacio Jones

"Survivors of abuse show us the strength of their personal spirit every time they smile."
— Jeanne McElvaney, Healing Insights: Effects of Abuse for Adults Abused as Children

"In situations of captivity, the perpetrator becomes the most powerful person in the life of the victim, and the psychology of the victim is shaped by the actions and beliefs of the perpetrator."
— Judith Lewis Herman, Trauma and Recovery: The Aftermath of Violence – From Domestic Abuse to Political Terror

"It is strange... the reasons one feels he doesn't deserve things."
— C. Kennedy, Slaying Isidore's Dragons

"In order to believe clients' accounts of trauma, you need to suspend any preconceived notions that you have about what is possible and impossible in human experience. As simple as they may sound, it may be difficult to do so."
— Aphrodite Matsakis, Post-Traumatic Stress Disorder

"If the abuser is a parent or caretaker, the abuse may be the most attention the child has had from that person. To the child, withholding attention can be a powerful form of coercion. Sexual molestation may be accompanied by physical expressions of affection that are sometimes the only affection the child receives."
— Rick Moskovitz, Lost in the Mirror: An Inside Look at Borderline Personality Disorder

"Walking away from someone you love is not an immoral thing. If that person isn't good for your wellbeing in any way, it's important to step away from that relationship."
— Arien Smith

"People expect all stories of abuse to be loud and angry but they're not. Sometimes they're quiet and cruel and swept under the rug."
— Trista Mateer, Aphrodite Made Me Do It

"Over the years, I had come to understand many things, but one was the clearest of all: you can survive anything if only you have one true friend."
— Meara O'Hara, The Wanderess and her Suitcase

"I thought that the world did not want me, but the truth was that I did not want myself."
— M.M. van der Reijden, Winter Magnolia

"The reason why you need emotional support is because it's important for survivors to be heard. To be understood. To be able to express yourself without fearing criticism or harsh judgment. To be validated for your pain, suffering, and loss. For others to be there for you to encourage you, especially if you're having a bad day or feeling triggered."
— Dana Arcuri, Soul Cry: Releasing & Healing the Wounds of Trauma

"My pain has always deserved a voice and I will not deny it, but I won't devote my life to it either."
— Trista Mateer, Aphrodite Made Me Do It

Help is available.
(Correct at time of publishing, UK)

Victim Support: 08081689111 – www.victimsupport.org.uk
A national charity dedicated to helping anyone affected by crime – not just victims and witnesses, but friends, family and anyone else caught up in the aftermath.
Rape Crisis: 08088029999 – www.rapecrisis.org.uk
A national charity offering confidential help, advice and a range of Rape Crisis Centres around the UK.
Galop: 08009995428 – www.galop.org.uk A national charity providing advice and support to members of the LGBT community.
Survivors UK: 02035983898 – www.survivorsuk.org A national charity supporting men who have been raped or sexually assaulted.
Crimestoppers: 0800555111 – www.crimestoppers-uk.org
A national charity with a free helpline for reporting crime anonymously.
Refuge: 08082000247 – www.refuge.org.uk Refuge supports women, children and men with a range of services, including refuges, independent advocacy, community outreach and culturally specific services.
Women's Aid: www.womansaid.org.uk Women's aid is a national charity working to end domestic abuse against women and children.
Men's Advice Line: 08088010327 – www.mensadviceline.org.uk Confidential helpline for men experiencing domestic violence.

If you are in an abusive relationship or someone you know is, seek help. Call the police if you or someone you know is in immediate danger, or your National Domestic Abuse helpline. Learning what help is available, and how to access it can save someone's life.

About the Author

Stephen Cooke is an abuse survivor and a trained Gas engineer with other qualifications including Computing, business, law and abuse recognition. This book, What is abuse is the first in a series of books dealing with domestic abuse from the perspective of a survivor.

Having met his first partner in approximately 1996, Stephen who was studying computer science and hoping for a career in microchip development was constantly hiding the scars and scratches from physical attacks he substatined. Unfortunately due to growing up in a working single parent household, Stephen's experience of family life was quite isolated and believed it when told this behavior was normal. In fact this behavior was also shown within her immediate family. Hostility, fights and abuse were rampant in their closed social environment. It was commonplace to be physical, emotionally abusive and make threats on an almost daily basis.

Stephen was later subjected to isolation tactics and married in a small ceremony to avoid any fights or drama which were normal in or after family gatherings. His ex partner would often blame external influences on her rages and outright unbelievable behavior. Mentally degrading, assaults and name-calling were commonplace and serious arguments happened 3-4 times a week. These were often blamed directly on her depression, her family or friends who were 'stirring the pot'. Her aggression I can only compare to that of a narcissist, although this was never officially confirmed due to her consistent lying. Stephen was fired from one of his jobs due to having to keep coming home to reassure his wife and calm down her rages. She completely refused to seek help, and unfortunately her family would back her up, saying she was not in the wrong and it was all someone else's fault.

In 2015, Stephen suffered stage 3 head and neck cancer. This along with the abuse at home left him with serious memory drops where he would be left almost completely helpless. After this, Stephen had to retire from his profession as a Gas Engineer. This left him in a victim's worst nightmare. Trapped with an abuser, no way out, no one to help and reliant on them. Stephen, being unaware of the fact his home life was domestic abuse, coupled with his confusion and short term memory loss attempted to take his own life.

After this, he started to reach out and made contact with the founder of the charity, Break the Silence. They made him aware of what was happening and helped him cope mentally. In 2018, after a prolonged period of abuse Stephen separated from his partner but stayed living together (for the children!). During the 2 years of cohabiting, Stephen had to move into the conservatory so he could physically lock the door away from her rages and aggression. During this time he called the police a number of times due to her physical and mental abuse, which had also shifted quite dramatically towards the children. But nothing was ever done. Stephen, unfortunately discovered the system, as well as some individuals were quite ignorant of abuse towards males.

Then in May 2020, after witnessing his daughter and how the abuse was directly affecting her, asked his ex wife to leave. She did and things remained somewhat 'ok' for a few weeks. But after his wife got others to start abusing their son, Stephen had cut off all contact for their safety and told her to seek a CAO so safeguarding protections could be put in place. Stephen got full custody and contact with their mother was left to the discretion of the children. His ex wife decided to call the police after Stephen safeguarded the children, claiming the very things she was doing. The police then immediately arrested him. This was unfounded and again Stephen witnessed first hand the bias of the system towards males. Stephen was not even allowed to report her to the police for domestic abuse, because she had reported him first.

Stephen now focuses his time helping victims of domestic abuse, raising awareness on all types of abuse and boundaries after trauma. This he does with the continued support of his friends and family, even though he still suffers with mind drops, which are triggered by his traumatic past.

To this day his ex wife has no 'official' record of any type linking her to being a perpetrator of abuse. Stephen's opinion in cases where the perpetrator cannot be identified for whatever reason, is that both parties should have details stored on the police national computer to allow for information sharing and Clare's Law requests.

Lightning Source UK Ltd.
Milton Keynes UK
UKHW020904100822
407113UK00010BB/1703